W9-CMP-357

NEW MINI

Second edition

Other books by this author:

Boreham
The 40-year story of Ford's
motorsport dream factory

Cosworth
The Search for Power

Ford in Touring Car Racing
Top of the class for fifty years

Transit
The 40-year story of Britain's
best-loved van

The Works Escorts

NEW
MINI
Second edition

RE04 XFV

GRAHAM ROBSON

First edition published in April 2002
Reprinted September 2002 (twice)
Second edition published in April 2005

A catalogue record for this book is
available from the British Library

ISBN 1 84425 135 7

Library of Congress catalog card no. 2004 117162

Haynes North America Inc.,
861 Lawrence Drive, Newbury Park,
California 91320, USA

Published by Haynes Publishing, Sparkford,
Yeovil, Somerset BA22 7JJ, UK
Tel: 01963 442030 Fax: 01963 440001
Int. tel: +44 1963 442030 Int. fax: +44 1963 440001
E-mail: sales@haynes.co.uk
Website: www.haynes.co.uk

Page layout by G&M Designs Limited,
Raunds, Northamptonshire
Printed and bound in Britain by
J. H. Haynes & Co. Ltd, Sparkford

Contents

Introduction

There were times when I wondered why I was writing a book about the new MINI, for the new model seems to bring controversy with it. For every classic Mini-owner ready to love the restatement of an old ideal, there are diehards ready to condemn the new car before they have even sat in one.

Millions of people, out there, are convinced that the only way to replace an original Issigonis-type Mini is to build another one. On the other hand BMW, who now own the brand, are sure that *their* painstakingly developed alternative was the only practical way to tackle the task.

For years, in the late 1990s, many of us knew that a new-generation MINI was on the way. After all those years, we accepted that as inevitable. Accordingly, it was only after BMW sold off Rover, but retained the MINI brand, that I realised how much it must mean to them. If this large German multi-national car-maker, which no longer had anything to prove, was ready to sink so much into a new motor car, *and* to start selling it in the world's most competitive market place – the United States – I knew that there was a story to tell.

Cars like this do not develop themselves. What follows is not merely a trawl through existing press material, and the second-guessing of other opinions, but my own deep research into the origins of the new MINI. The story, which really began in 1993, is neither simple nor a fairy tale – but it shows how a famous marque survived in the face of awful financial and commercial crises. It shows how (and why) it needed mighty financial muscle, and stubborn resolve, to bring it to the market place.

It is, I hope, the definitive story of the birth of a vitally important new car. Yet this is not a complete story. One year, two years, three years into the future, there will be more MINIS on sale – and BMW hopes that this saga will run and run for decades to come.

Meeting a phenomenon

It was a wet November Friday, and the British traffic was awful. I was faced with driving the new MINI, for the first time, in bad-tempered commuter traffic. To meet the new MINI Cooper I had already driven for 150 miles in an air-conditioned, leather-upholstered Jaguar, and the contrast was worrying me. It was not the ideal way to be introduced to a controversial new car.

I need not have worried. The Cooper was quick, comfortable, well-equipped – and everyone else seemed to be smiling at me. Of course, I should have expected this. Here was a new car which the British public was willing itself to love. In the past I had owned Minis, they had owned Minis – in fact almost everyone I know seemed to have driven a Mini at one time or another.

All of them, all of us, and especially myself, wanted to know what the new car was all about. All of us had old Mini memories tucked away in our minds. The first time we'd driven one ... the first time

Unmistakeable from any angle, and with so many obvious cues to earlier Minis, the new MINI had the sort of face that seemed to make everyone smile. (David Wigmore)

6

Like the original Mini of 1959, the BMW-inspired Mini of 2001 was a squat little car, with a wheel at each corner.

we'd taken out our future partners in one … the first time we'd learned about front-wheel-drive … the first time we'd raced one … the first time we'd out-driven a far faster car in one … the first time we'd discovered just what a damned fine little machine it was … and the first time we'd realised that we spent all the time scooting round with a big grin on our faces.

So, here I was, ready to learn the truth. Was the new Mini a *real* Mini like the old one? Did it do all the same things? Did it steer as well, did it handle as well? How did it perform? How did it compare with an icon of the 1960s? In other words, did it deserve to carry that immortal badge – Mini?

Like everyone else, I was impatient to find out, for here was a new car which seemed to have been on the way for decades.

Earlier attempts to replicate Alec Issigonis's masterpiece had failed, so why should this one be different? Anyway, even this, the definitely-in-production Mini, seemed to have been imminent for a long time.

Impress me, I thought. I've been waiting for years to see if anyone could do what Alec Issigonis had done in 1959. Prove to me that you really *have* the Mini's genes in your pedigree. Has it really been worth the wait?

I need not have worried. Although the pre-launch hype had been unsurpassed, I soon decided that the new Mini was a fine little car, and I could see why other motoring writers had fallen for it. I could rest easy. Even though I originally wondered why it was so much bigger than real Minis should be, and it took time for

me to accept that it was now being built by a German concern, I soon accepted it as a twenty-first century technical statement.

Grateful thanks

BMW, no doubt, might have preferred me to write this book without referring to the past, but since Rover (which they sold in 2000) was so important to the genesis of the MINI, I could not do that. Because both companies know that I have talked to the other, I am especially grateful to everyone for being so free with information, assistance and good old-fashioned encouragement.

BMW, the parent company, and since 1994 the controller of the MINI brand, has helped me enormously with facts, facilities, interviews, illustrations and, of course, the loan of a MINI.

From BMW in Germany, I need to thank Gert Hildebrand, Sonja Ott, Torsten Muller-Oetvoes, Dr Heinrich Petra and Sandra Schillmoeller.

From BMW in the UK, my grateful thanks go to: Dr Herbert Diess, Ellysia Graymore, Mark Harrison, Jane Marjoram, Angela Wigley and Chris Willows.

From BMW in the USA: Mike McHale.

From Rover in the UK many personalities gave of their memories, including Brian Griffin, Chris Lee, Dave Saddington and Geoff Upex, while Kevin Jones and Sarah Chamberlayne helped enormously with pictures and facts.

Peter Minnis and Helen Webster (of the authoritative British *MINI MAGAZINE*) were generous in providing pictures of important old Minis, Ian Elliott dug deep to find me a colour illustration of the old Mini Metro and Don Racine (of Mini Mania in the USA) helped with illustrations of what future motorsport MINIS might look like.

Photographs were supplied as follows: MG Rover – pages 27, 28, 29, 41, 42, 43, 44, 45, 46, 47, 55, 80, 81, 98. Mini Mania – page 131. Robson archive – pages 13, 15, 17, 18, 19, 20, 21, 22, 23, 24, 25, 26, 31, 32, 87, 101. The rest, except where

credited separately, are from BMW.

Then, of course, there is my good friend Gary Anderson of San Jose, California, long-time editor of *British Car* magazine, who seems to know where any and every motoring enthusiast in that vast continent actually lives. Only he knows how he has helped me so much.

The most valued contribution came at a later stage, in unpromising British weather conditions, when David Wigmore's skill with cameras produced stunning photography of a MINI Cooper.

I really could not have finished this job without the help of all these people – and I will always be in their debt. I am grateful to them all.

GRAHAM ROBSON

The new MINI is a brand, all on its own, and not merely a model of any other make. The badges on the new car make this very clear.
(David Wigmore)

Evolution –
a 40-year process

From the introduction of the original Mini in 1959, to the launch of the first new-model MINIS for sale in 2001 and 2002.

1959 Introduction of the original 848cc-engined, front-wheel-drive Mini.

1964 Paddy Hopkirk's Mini-Cooper S won the Monte Carlo Rally. The Mini's sporting legend was confirmed.

1967 Work started on 9X – a smaller, lighter, replacement-Mini project, with a hatchback body style, and a new overhead-camshaft engine. Work cancelled in 1969.

1972 Systematic studies made for improvement of the existing Mini, with major body changes, but no mechanical improvements.

1972 Development of the ADO74 project, larger than the Mini, with an overhead-camshaft engine. Cancelled in 1974.

1973 Project work began on ADO88. Meant as a Mini-replacement, but unlike ADO74, still to use the existing A-Series Mini engine and transmission.

1974 Introduction of Bertone-styled Innocenti Mini, to be made in Italy. Never manufactured or marketed in UK.

1977 ADO88 revamped, as LC8, with the same platform, and engine, but with enlarged cabin.

1980 LC8 introduced to the public as the Mini Metro.

1994 Low-budget work produced Minki Two – a wider and longer Mini, with the K-Series engine. A one-off.

1995 BMW approved the E50 project, for the development of a new MINI. To have an all-new platform, 16-valve engine and style. To be built at the Rover Group plant at Longbridge.

10

1996	E50 Mini project handed over to the Rover Group for finalisation. Became R50 at this time.
1997	Brief official glimpse of the new Mini, on the eve of the Frankfurt Motor Show. No technical details released at that time.
1999	Responsibility for Mini project taken back to Germany.
March 2000	BMW decided to sell the Rover Group, but retain the Mini brand. Decision made to build new Mini at Oxford. At the same time, Rover 75 assembly to be moved from Oxford to Longbridge.
October 2000	New-generation Mini finally launched at Paris Salon. Production to begin in 2001, sales in mid-2001.
April 2001	Volume production of new Mini began in Oxford.
July 2001	Sales of Mini began in the UK. Sales in Europe followed in September 2001.
October 2001	Mini Cooper S previewed, for sale in 2002.
Spring 2002	Mini sales began in the USA.
July 2002	Mini Cooper S sales began.

June 2003	Diesel-engined Mini One went on sale.
May 2003	Mini featured in new *Italian Job* movie.
April 2004	100,000th UK-market Mini delivered.

Range revisions included Getrag instead of Rover gearbox for One and Cooper, more power for Cooper S, and minor front-end facelift, with equipment enhancement for all types.

July/ August 2004	Launch of Convertible style, in One, Cooper, and Cooper S derivatives.
25 August 2004	500,000th Mini produced at Oxford.

In December 2004, BMW and Peugeot revealed the new 16-valve 1.6-litre engine which will power the Mini from 2006.

1 False starts

Replacing a legend

Replacing an icon is always difficult. To do that, you need time, money and resolve – and for many years those who owned the Mini brand could not assemble all of them. Time and again, forceful managers and engineers would dabble, sketch and maybe even build a prototype, but there would be no end result.

Forty-two years after Alec Issigonis's brilliant motoring concept first appeared, a new-generation MINI finally went on sale. Bigger, faster and altogether more complex than the original had ever been, it was the result of five years' toil from Rover Group (who had inherited the brand after several takeovers, rescues and reconstructions) and from BMW, who had provided truckloads of money. BMW, of course, had bought the Rover Group and thereby inherited the Mini brand in 1994.

Even so, it was a tortuous business. Conceived in 1995, first glimpsed in public in 1997 and finally launched in 2000, the new car – called MINI, the use of capital letters being important – was the latest of many projects which had all set out to do the same. Because Issigonis's original had been so successful – right for its job, right for its market – to improve on it had sometimes seemed to be Mission Impossible. Issigonis, arrogant, dogmatic and self-centred though he was, inspired this one great achievement. At a stroke, no question, he completely changed the shape of the motor car.

Before the Mini, front-wheel-drive cars

were seen to be eccentric, for in the 1950s rear-engined cars were dominant: front-wheel-drive cars with transverse engines were unknown. Even later, when more and more British Motor Corporation cars adopted the same layout, it took time for the message to sink in. Then came the Peugeot 204, the Fiat 128 and the VW Golf – after which no other layout seemed to fit the bill.

The original ADO15 Mini (ADO was an acronym for Austin Drawing Office) was conceived at BMC in 1957 – to satisfy chairman Sir Leonard Lord's desire for a fuel-efficient little car to crush the rash of bubble cars which spread across Europe in the wake of the first Suez War. Except that he insisted on the use of an existing BMC engine, Sir Leonard was ready to indulge Issigonis's every whim, the result being these tiny (120in long), stubby and amazingly versatile two-door saloons which went on sale in August 1959.

Because scores of books have already profiled what we now call the 'Classic Mini', I need only summarise the car's layout, appeal – and shortcomings. The layout consisted of a transversely-mounted engine, a gearbox mounted under it (effectively in the sump) and front-wheel-drive featuring Constant Velocity Joints which had evolved from military submarine conning tower control technology. Inch-accurate steering was by rack-and-pinion, the wheels were tiny (the tyre section was 5.20-10in) and there was very firm all-

According to BMC, in 1959, you could stow all this baggage, and a load of passengers, in the Mini.

independent suspension by rubber cone springs. Not only were these the world's smallest possible four-seater saloons, but also they handled like tiny tin-top go-karts, and seemed to appeal to all classes of society. The fact that the build quality of early cars was abysmal (jokes about carpets floating away in wet weather, because of leaks, were well-founded), and that because of the near-vertical steering column layout, and crudely-engineered seats, the driving position generated gainful employment for hundreds of osteopaths, was soon forgotten and sales rocketed to astonishing levels.

And for why? Not because the new Mini was so economical, nor because it was so durable – but because it was such fun to drive. John Cooper, that legendary motor racing character who inspired the birth of the original Mini-Cooper, summed up

everything with two favourite stories. In one, he described the new car as: 'Like Dr Who's Tardis – as small as a phone box outside, as big as the Albert Hall inside.' More vividly, he recalled lending an early Mini to a noted Italian race car designer at Monza, who disappeared for a test drive in frantic Italian traffic. Returning, obviously shaken, he tossed the keys to Cooper with a wry smile and the comment: 'If it wasn't so ugly, I would shoot myself!'

Pop stars loved Minis, princesses drove around in them, film star Peter Sellers had a special version built as a town car and the Beatles were pictured with them. The Mini-Cooper, and especially the Mini-Cooper S, became rally winners and giant-killing racing cars. Engines eventually grew from 848cc to 1,275cc, and power outputs soared from 34bhp to 76bhp. There was nothing, it seemed, that a Mini could not do.

Alec Issigonis's original Mini changed the face of motoring – for ever. With a transverse engine, front-wheel-drive and these cheeky looks, it was a real trend-setter. (David Wigmore/MINI MAGAZINE)

Annual production soon exceeded 200,000, with BMC originally building cars on two sites – at Longbridge, near Birmingham, and at Cowley, near Oxford. Both will have important roles in the story which has to be told. The millionth Mini was produced in 1965, Riley and Wolseley versions were launched, while estate cars and tiny panel vans were added to the range. Hydrolastic suspension was introduced in 1964, an automatic transmission option followed in 1965 and a slightly face-lifted style was scheduled for 1967. Already the Mini was the best-selling British car of all time.

It all sounded like a fairy tale, but behind the scenes it was not. Despite the numbers being manufactured (at this time, one of every three BMC cars being built was a Mini) the Mini was not actually making any money. Publicly, at least, BMC never admitted to this, though it meant that they were not generating the cash flow needed to invest in new models.

Sir Leonard's successor, Sir George Harriman, never reacted to this – not by raising prices and profit margins. Not even BMC's deadly rivals, Ford, could convince him that he had a problem. Terry Beckett, who would become Ford-UK's chairman, recalls: 'As soon as the Mini came out ... I could see straight away that it was of such complexity that there was no way that they could be producing it for there to be any profit ... Two weeks later, we bought one and stripped it right down to the spot welds. We examined every part – and there wasn't any way they could be making money.'

Ford's long-serving chairman, Sir Patrick Hennessy, then called Sir George, told him that BMC could go bust if it did not raise

The Mini Cooper S was a great competition car – this was Paddy Hopkirk on the way to winning the Monte Carlo Rally in 1964.

Alec Issigonis's 9X, designed in 1967/1968, could have been the 'new Mini', if British Leyland had not cancelled it. Shorter than the classic Mini, it would have had a new overhead-camshaft engine. (David Wigmore/MINI MAGAZINE)

prices and that Ford would follow them if it tried to match them. Yet Harriman was arrogant enough to insist that he was a production specialist and knew what he was doing.

9X – Mini, the second time around

Although BMC was usually profitable, it rarely made enough to invest hugely in new products. Years were spent replicating the Mini formula, on a larger scale – the 1100, the 1800 and the awful Maxi – and in fleshing out its marques by developing

'badge-engineered' versions. This was a time when Issigonis became BMC's Technical Director, and when his word on new models was rarely queried. When he evolved his vision for BMC's future, he envisaged the development of a new range of related overhead-camshaft four-cylinder and six-cylinder engines, all in newly-engineered transverse-engined cars with front-wheel-drive. As for the Product Planning department – there is little evidence that he ever took notice, and we now know they were terrified of him …

When Issigonis decided that he should

start to renew the entire product range, his first priority was a new Mini. Many Issigonis-watchers found this inevitable. One of his closest associates told me: 'The Mini was his one "great idea", and he wanted to be remembered for it. Every other BMC car which followed was bigger, heavier and somehow less "pure". He wasn't really interested in them. He only really enjoyed working on Minis …'

In 1967, therefore, the still-independent BMC management encouraged him to put the first part of his master plan into existence – at least in prototype form. Cloistered away with just six hand-picked engineers in self-contained workshops, he finally set out to produce a Mini-replacement. This was 9X, the first of several 'pie-in-the-sky' schemes which would splutter into life over the years.

9X, Issigonis decided, would not only have a new structure and a new engine, but would also have new suspension. His target was to make 9X smaller, lighter and at least five per cent cheaper to build than the existing Mini. With no limits yet set on

capital spending, or on technological innovation, this was an audacious target. 9X, therefore, was to be brand-new from end-to-end and tip-to-toe – and would have required colossal investment to put on sale.

Amazingly, one 9X has survived, and is usually on display at the British Motor Industry Heritage Trust (BMIHT) museum at Gaydon, in Warwickshire. Crucially, there were few carryover parts from the existing car – perhaps just the tiny 10in wheels. The structure was new, with sharper and more angular lines, and there were no exposed body seams.

9X had fresh, crisp, proportions, the wheels being at each corner, and the bonnet extremely short. Because the overall width had crept up to 58.5in, the cabin was slightly larger than that of the Mini. There was more glass, and a new type of 'half-hatchback' feature, with a lift-up rear window, but with a deep and sturdy cross-panel below it.

Issigonis had personally influenced the proportions, though the style was certainly influenced by BMC's favoured consultant,

Some of the most fascinating historic Minis are at the BMIHT Museum at Gaydon, in Warwickshire. Here are the three Monte Carlo Rally winning cars (1964, 1967 and 1965) on a special display.

The
Issigonis
legacy

If Morris Minor designer Alec Issigonis had not joined the British Motor Corporation (BMC) in 1956, if the Suez War had not erupted in October of the same year, if petrol shortages had not ensued and if BMC had not suddenly seen the demand for a new type of ultra-small car, the 'Mini' as we know it might never have evolved.

But it did, and the world of motoring was changed – for ever. Except that he was obliged to use an existing small BMC engine, Issigonis was given a completely free hand to design what he liked. As his second masterpiece (the Morris Minor had been his first), Issigonis therefore conceived a car so small that four-seater accommodation seemed not to be possible.

But it was. Choosing a compact transverse engine/front-wheel-drive package and (important, this) tiny 10in wheels, Issigonis provided a miniature saloon where 80 per cent of the volume was given over to accommodation – seating and stowage. The 'Mini' was given the only possible name which would suit.

Styling? Issigonis himself did not believe that 'his' cars needed to be shaped, but his chairman (Sir Leonard Lord) did not agree. Accordingly, though the shape was indeed very simple, it was refined by the Nuffield design team at Cowley – for 'cues' shared with other 1950s Morris models are obvious.

Tinier cars had already been built (the Fiat 500 of 1957 was one such), but none had such efficient packaging. Early on, willing students risked asphyxiation by trying to set new records for the number of people who could be packed inside the car with the doors and windows closed.

It was not, in other words, that the Mini had front-wheel-drive, but that it was so efficiently drawn. To compete, every other mini, or super-mini, which followed, had to match this. Thus it was that Issigonis, perhaps the first automotive designer ever to put passengers' needs before engineering, arranged his legacy in one hit.

This barrel-sided Mini, with a slightly more capacious cabin, was one of several schemes tried out in the early 1970s.

Pininfarina. I can definitely see some of the same 'cues' as in the Peugeot 104, which was also Pininfarina-influenced, and contemporary.

Interestingly, although 9X was four inches *shorter* than the Mini, its wheelbase was four inches longer. This, allied to the ultra-short bonnet, meant that the cabin was longer, with a less bus-like driving position. There was even less front and rear overhang, there was no sign of the Mini's original bulky sub-frames and the suspension was by conventional steel springs – MacPherson struts at the front, and Peugeot-type transverse torsion bars at the rear.

The engine, though, provided all the novelties. The first of a proposed new family – four or six-cylinder, 750cc to 1,300cc, all with aluminium heads, cast-iron blocks, single overhead camshaft/cogged belt drive valve gear and two valves per cylinder – it was a 43bhp/850cc unit.

The electric alternator was built in to the main mass of the flywheel, and the transmission (still under the engine, rather than end-on to it), was now to be a simpler two-shaft design. This astonishing little power unit was not only 25 per cent more efficient than the Mini's A-Series but, complete with transmission, weighed only 200lb/91kg, which was a 40 per cent

reduction on the A-Series pack, which weighed 340lb/154kg. A 'stretch' to 1,000cc was feasible. Many of the features of this engine would influence the birth of Rover Group's celebrated K-Series, which followed two decades later.

The new engine was so small, and the 9X engine bay was built so cosily round it, that prototype cars could not possibly have run with A-Series engines instead. That, in a way, was the project's undoing, as otherwise a half-way house might have been acceptable to the accountants.

Two 9X prototypes were completed, then cancelled. Astonishingly, the programme was not formally abandoned until 1977. Unhappily for Issigonis, it evolved at the same time as BMH (BMC had joined forces with Jaguar) merged with Leyland in 1968, to form British Leyland. When Leyland's hierarchy walked into Longbridge in May 1968, they were astonished to find no sign

of Issigonis in the main engineering department. When eventually discovered, his new Mini was at once assessed, his engine's master plan was abandoned and all impetus behind 9X was lost.

For Issigonis, the apparent genius who could do no wrong for BMC, the capital costs required never seemed to be an issue. For British Leyland, once they had seen the new car which had been designed, it became the only issue.

Although the first 9X was completed in 1968/1969, little testing ever took place. Harry Webster (ex-Standard-Triumph technical chief) took over as technical director of the newly-named Austin-Morris Division in May 1968. Despite the fact that orders went out for 9X to be scrapped, Issigonis and his loyal associates, insubordinate to the last, made sure that the hardware was instead stored away, and preserved.

'My name is Michael Caine …' – our hero with a late-model Mini, commemorating the huge part that a trio of Mini Cooper S cars had in his film, The Italian Job.

The Bertone-styled Innocenti Mini appeared in 1974, using a standard Mini platform, and all the running gear. Tens of thousands were sold in Italy – and in the late 1970s it was re-engined with a Daihatsu power train.

Conceived in 1974 as a Mini replacement, but introduced in 1980 as an extra model, the Mini Metro used Mini engines and transmissions, but a unique platform. It finally ended its career in 1998, as the Rover 100.

Soon after this, Alec Issigonis was finally sidelined, being given the rather nebulous title of Director of Research and Development, and never again influenced mainstream design at Longbridge.

Early 1970s Mini replacements

From late 1972 to early 1974, in parallel with ADO74 (which I describe next), studies were made for a 'Classic Mini replacement', which would have used an existing Mini platform – in either 80in (saloon) wheelbase or 84in (estate car) wheelbase – with a new three-door body style. Seven different stages of development were studied, the schemes gradually growing from 120in to 125in overall length, and from 55.9in to 59in wide.

New outer skin panels would have been used (this was a classic 're-skin'), to include curved side glasses, both for doors and rear

quarter windows, all to provide a more generous interior package.

All schemes retained the existing Mini A-Series engine/transmission layout, but with a front-mounted radiator. Initially, existing Mini subframes were retained, but later schemes used ADO67/Austin Allegro rear suspension instead.

No prototypes were actually built.

ADO74

The next full-scale attempt to replace the Mini came in the early 1970s, when British Leyland's strategy was already in disarray. Coded ADO74, this project was always envisaged as a slightly larger car, to replace the latest long-nose Mini, the Mini Clubman and 1275GT types, which had been introduced in 1969.

From June 1972 to March 1974, much styling and engineering effort went into this car. It was intended to use a brand-new overhead camshaft K-Series engine (not yet the same as the K-Series which eventually went on sale at the end of the 1980s), which had evolved from the earlier H-Series, of which prototypes ran for 25,000 road test miles, and 800 test bed hours.

ADO74 was larger, even, than the long-nosed Mini Clubman (it was much closer, in fact, to the size of the 2001 MINI). In this design the 8-valve/overhead-camshaft K-Series would have been of 1,100cc or 1,300cc, transversely mounted, and steeply inclined back towards the passenger bulkhead, with a five-speed transmission behind it. The new car was to have an 88in/2,235mm wheelbase, with MacPherson strut front suspension and coil spring independent rear suspension.

This is a comparison of ADO74 with the short-nose Classic Mini:

Feature	ADO74	Classic Mini
Length	138in	120in
Wheelbase	88in	80in
Width	61.5in	55.5in
Height	52.0in	51.5in
Front/rear wheel tracks	52/52in	48/46in
Wheel size	12in	10in

A seriously researched programme, it progressed as far as styling clays and package drawings: a single bare body shell was built. A style theme was already chosen, and engineering development was about to begin when, in March 1974, it was discovered that £130 million would be needed to get the new car and the new engine into production – this being money that British Leyland did not have.

Overhead-camshaft conversions of existing engines

A-Series: To minimise the cost of new engine investment, single-overhead-camshaft conversions of the ageing A-Series power unit were developed in the mid-1970s. These featured simple, vertical, eight-valve layouts, the cylinder heads being aluminium, with camshaft drive by internally cogged belt.

Three engine sizes – 970cc, 1,097cc and 1,275cc – were proposed, and developed in prototype form, the test bed power being 59bhp (970cc) to 84bhp (1,275cc). No fewer than 2,000 test bed hours were completed, along with 2,200 miles in various test cars.

Three-cylinder E-Series: The conventional four-cylinder E-Series was an overhead-camshaft type being used in Austin Maxi (from 1969) and Allegro (from 1973) models, with slightly inclined inlet and exhaust valves, driven via fingers. With improved packaging and lighter weight in mind, three-cylinder varieties were investigated in 1975 – a 1,750cc 'four' therefore becoming a 1,300cc 'three'.

Studies showed that 970cc and 1,300cc three-cylinder engines could certainly have been refined, and would have been short enough to have mated with the desired 'end-on' gearbox in a new model.

Innocenti – the Italian Job

In the meantime, in a development which confused Mini-watchers for years, an Italian giant, and a related styling house (Bertone), had got in on the act. Innocenti, with large factories in Italy, were business associates of British Leyland (who had recently taken financial control), and had been assembling conventional Minis under licence for some years. Suddenly, at the Turin Motor Show of November 1974, they showed a new model, which they christened the Innocenti Mini.

Original-shape Metro prototypes, still known as ADO88s, had less shapely bodies, with flatter sides. This car is seen brake testing, complete with disguise at the front to change the shape of the car.

Original Metros were all three-door cars, but a neat five-door version was later conceived. This was the original stylist's interpretation.

British Leyland approved of this project – they were to supply under-body platforms and all the running gear for the model – and at first there were rumours that this was also a kite-flying exercise from home. Not so – for Innocenti, in cahoots with Bertone, had gained British Leyland's approval to start this as a private-enterprise project. Even so, the British magazine *Autocar*'s reaction was typical of press speculation: 'It is to be hoped that something of the kind may form the basis for an eventual Mini successor, though we should not be disappointed that this newcomer is only for the Italian market ...'

Innocenti had the size, the capability and the industrial muscle to commission its own pressed-steel body shell and tooling, but not to evolve the style, so it had turned to Bertone for that. Limited by the need to use virtually unmodified Mini platform and bulkhead assemblies, plus the well known A-Series engine, transmission and running gear (though Mini 1275GT-type 12in wheels were adopted), this specialist house then completed a remarkable styling job around a totally new superstructure.

The overall length was 123in – just three inches longer than the original Mini – while the width had crept up to 59in, which was 3.5 inches wider. Not only were the lines altogether smarter and more crisp than those of the original, but this time there was a rear hatchback/third-door, and folding rear seats. Superficially, there were similarities to the 9X layout (which had been inspired by Pininfarina).

Innocenti produced this car in 998cc '90' and 1,275cc '120' form – both engines being allied to a front-mounted water radiator with an electric fan. Both had far more luxurious equipment than the standard cars being built in the UK, and on the 120 models there was a full-width fascia, featuring face-level ventilation, front seats could be reclined and a rear wiper/wash was standard.

Although these pretty little cars were, admittedly, no more spacious than the originals, and were considerably more expensive, they had a great deal of panache and soon began to sell very well. So, why was the Bertone style not adopted at Longbridge – if only as an optional model?

Senior British Leyland designer/stylist Rex Fleming, later to be much involved in the Mini Metro project, told me that: 'We had a good look at the idea of using the

Bertone style, or a development of it, and there were various ways it could have been done. The style, as a style, appealed to us, but that was all.

Rex's associate, Harris Mann, added more detail: 'The problem was the seating package. There was not more, but less, room inside than in a Mini, and that would never have done. Charles Griffin [who had recently become Director of Engineering] had laid down a minimum package for the new car, and the Bertone was a long way off.'

British interest in the Bertone Mini, therefore, died almost as soon as it had been born. Although British Leyland imported a few cars, and considered their use very carefully, the idea of transplanting assembly to the UK was soon abandoned. The Bertone-styled car, though, went on to a long and distinguished career. After British Leyland's bankruptcy in 1975, Innocenti was bought by Alejandro De Tomaso (whose other interests already included Maserati). From 1976 the Mini was re-badged as the 'De Tomaso Mini',

and carried on strongly. Years later it was completely re-engineered, to use a Daihatsu power pack, though the Mini platform and suspension layouts were always retained.

The Mini Metro project

Started in 1974, launched in 1980, re-badged as a Rover in 1994 and not finally dropping out of production at Longbridge until the end of 1998, this was the first 'Mini replacement' which ever made it all the way from 'Good idea' to 'Showroom' status. Like all previous attempts, however, it was not a direct replacement for a much-loved car – for the Issigonis Mini carried on, alongside it, throughout its long career,

The Mini Metro of 1980 was a carefully packed front-wheel-drive, considerably larger than the original Mini, but using the same A-Series engine/transmission, along with Hydragas suspension and a hatchback.

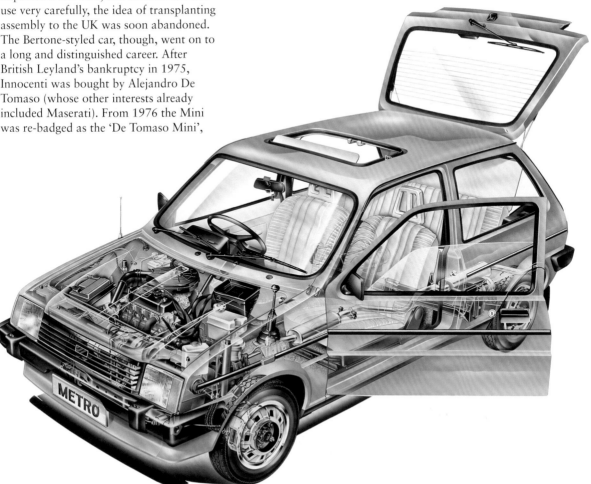

In 1990 the Mini Metro was facelifted, with a shapely new nose, which hid the new Rover K-Series overhead camshaft engine, and the R65 gearbox which would later be used in the MINI of 2001.

and outlived it. This, though, was a car which sold in millions, and which was cleared out of Longbridge (prematurely, as it transpired) to make way for the new MINI, and which was arguably a more versatile car than the Issigonis Mini had ever been.

Almost as soon as ADO74 had been cancelled in 1974, project work and 'why don't we …?' sessions began for its successor. This time, though, it was to be tackled without the luxury of developing a new engine/transmission, and above all it had to be completed inside a much tighter budget.

With Charles Griffin now in overall technical command of such projects, a new car, originally coded ADO88, got under way. Griffin's brief, particularly to his designer/stylists, was that ADO88 was to be little longer than the long-nose Mini Clubman. It should have a wheelbase of about 88in (which partly explains the use

of the ADO88 code), was initially to be a three-door hatchback and was to have the most spacious possible interior seating package. The car which went on sale would be 134in long, a full 14in longer than the Classic Mini. To quote Harris Mann: 'The most important Commandment that Charles handed down was: "Thou Shalt Not Lose Any Package" …'

Even after the financial traumas of 1975, when British Leyland had to be taken into Government ownership, ADO88 always looked likely to go ahead, and for a time its launch date was inked in for October 1978, though this hope soon slipped to 1979. Clay models prepared by the studio in 1974 changed little over the years – not, that is, until another management change caused the style to be made more bulbous, and the code to be changed to LC8 (where LC stood for Leyland Cars).

Having decided to re-use existing Mini power plants – A-Series engines, with a

choice of manual or automatic transmissions in the sump – the biggest decision to be made concerned suspension. Rubber cone and Hydrolastic suspension (both previously found on the Mini) were discarded in favour of the new Hydragas system, which was already adopted for the ADO67/Austin Allegro.

Settling the style took ages. Comparisons were made with the Bertone Mini, Pininfarina was invited to provide a theme, and there was a change of styling director, with David Bache (ex-Rover) arriving. Final exterior approval came in February 1976.

Ten early prototypes followed, and 24 further Fully Engineered Prototypes (FEPs) followed in 1977. All looked set – until more upsets hit the beleagured company. First, in August 1977, ADO88 was submitted to European clinics – where its 'plain-Jane' style was demonstrably not liked: 'The car was seen as having an excellent package and function,' Harris

Mann stated, 'but the style was seen as too austere, somewhat slab-sided and even a bit ugly around the rear end ...'

At the same time, British Leyland management was in disarray, with chairman Sir Richard Dobson forced to resign over indiscreet (some say, racist) remarks made at a private dinner. His replacement was the dynamic Sir Michael Edwardes. One of Sir Michael's first decisions was to have the ADO88 style revised.

But there was a big problem. Many of ADO88's major steel pressings – which included the entire floor pan, the interior door panels and other structural panels – had already been released for press tool construction to take place, and could therefore not be changed without incurring huge financial penalties. In a process which saw ADO88 become LC8, what was effectively a complete re-skin exercise was completed – in a mere six weeks!

Mini and Metro Cabriolets were both few and far between. Not only did the fold-back roofs look awkward, but they were a lot more expensive than the hatchbacks. BMW, however, seem certain to introduce a MINI Cabriolet in the 2000s.

Five million customers can't be wrong. The original-shape Mini reached that milestone in 1986, and British media star Noel Edmonds was there to commemorate the occasion.

'For the next six weeks,' says Harris Mann, 'I don't think I have ever worked so hard. It was almost like tackling the face-lift of a car which had already been on sale. But this job had to be finished in six weeks, no more, and even then we were sure that it was going to delay the launch.'

But the job was done, entirely in-house at Longbridge, final style approval came in December 1977, a further styling clinic (in

Paris) was a success and public launch was set for October 1980. So many leaks had already taken place that British Leyland therefore admitted its existence, and started calling it the 'Mighty Mini'.

This was the period when top management took a Very Brave Pill – deciding the LC8/Mighty Mini should not replace the Mini after all. Because the Classic Mini was still selling at 200,000 cars a year, it was decided to keep it going. Mighty Mini (soon to be christened 'Mini Metro') would also be assembled at Longbridge, would therefore replace the Mini Clubman/1275GT types and should carve out its own niche.

And so it was decided, and carried out. Ten new FEPs were built in 1978, then a further 40 PRVs (Proving Vehicles) followed in 1979. Compulsory crash tests were satisfactorily completed, and because the company's new proving ground at Gaydon, south of Warwick (it had once been an RAF V-bomber base) also came on stream in 1978–1979, millions of test miles were soon notched up.

New body manufacturing facilities were erected at Longbridge's West Works (west, that is, of the main building, and on the other side of the A38 trunk road). Delivery to the assembly lines was arranged by overhead conveyors, and new assembly lines were prepared in one of the main factory CAB (Car Assembly Building) monoliths, where up to 6,500 cars could be built every week. The A-Series engine was thoroughly re-vamped, and tens of millions were then spent on pre-launch leaks, fanfares, press launches and previews.

By the time the Mini Metro started to roll – in spite of a rash of strikes which regularly threatened BL – more than £300 million had been spent. In cash terms, this was more than ADO74 would have cost, but in the six years which separated them, rampant inflation had made a nonsense of comparisons.

The gamble of the Metro (and it certainly *was* a gamble) worked, and worked well. By 1981 the revamped

Longbridge plant was already producing 3,000 Metros every week, and this would eventually be eased up to 4,500 a week.

Yet the old dilemma – how to replace the Mini – remained. Although the Metro was an enduring success, it could not replace the Mini itself. Combined sales, though, shot up. In 1979, 165,500 Classic Minis were built, but in 1981 (after the Metro had appeared) that figure fell to only 70,000. In 1981, though, no fewer than 165,750 Metros were assembled – which meant a combined total of 235,750 – and the trends were still upwards.

The inevitable long-term result was that the Metro took many sales away from the Mini. With both cars sitting, side-by-side, in British Leyland showrooms, customers had to make a choice. Did they want a Classic Mini – cheap, small, cheeky, nippy,

but beginning to look old-fashioned? Or did they want a Metro, less sporty in character, and inevitably more expensive, but more roomy, with a practical hatchback feature and a higher-quality and more versatile interior?

For the Mini, unhappily, all the trends pointed one way – downwards. Although the five millionth car was produced in 1986, the fact is that annual production had already dropped to no more than 35,000 cars a year. Even though the company tried to keep up interest by producing a regular output of Special Edition models, it could not halt the decline.

Production figures tell their own story. After a brief resurgence in 1990 (to 46,000) when the Mini-Cooper was reintroduced and the Metro was taken further up-

The last Classic Mini of all was built at Longbridge in October 2000, more than 41 years after production had started. By that time a new-generation MINI had already been launched.

27

To show how things were changing at Longbridge in October 2000, MG-Rover chose to show the last Mini of all alongside the first off-the-line Rover 75, whose assembly had been moved from Oxford to make way for the new MINI. Managing Director Kevin Howe tells the story.

British pop star Lulu was on hand to greet the last-ever Classic Mini, when it was completed at Longbridge.

market, Mini production slumped to only 20,000 in 1993. Although exports to Japan were strong, British-market sales fell to 16,154 in 1986, to 10,067 in 1990 and to a miserable 6,326 in 1993.

In the face of such discouraging figures Rover (the company name which finally emerged from the wreckage of British Leyland/BL/Austin-Rover) elected to move the Metro up-market. By spending no less than £200 million, the structure was re-vamped (notably by widening the engine bay, and the chassis 'legs' which embraced it), to make it possible to insert the Rover 200's new overhead-camshaft K-series engine, complete with R65 transmission – instead of the ancient A-Series power unit. Although British prices therefore rocketed – in 1990 A-Series engined cars spanned £5,575–£7,765, whereas the new K-Series engined cars cost £5,985–£9,735 – these were significantly better cars, which felt altogether more mature.

That progress was carried on further (and finally) in December 1994, when, under BMW's tutelage, the Metro was face-lifted, and renamed Rover 100, which is how it ended its career in 1998.

Dilemma in the 1990s

As far as the old Mini was concerned, what ought to be done? Could such an icon ever be replaced? Was there still a market for a small, basically-equipped, car? Because annual sales had slumped so badly, was there even a business case for investing upwards of £300 million to develop a new-generation model?

Until the mid-1990s, whether it was BMC ... or British Leyland ... or Leyland Cars ... or Austin-Rover ... or the Rover Group, no management team had ever dared to tackle this dilemma. But now the brand was owned by the mighty BMW concern. Would everything now be different?

Pop star Lulu poses, but the final Mini takes most of the attention. Some assembly staff pictured here had worked on Mini assembly for the whole of their careers. The end, in Longbridge, was a bitter-sweet occasion for many of them.

2 Teasers in the 1990s
Spiritual and ACV30

If you had slipped, unobserved, into Rover Group's development areas in the early 1990s, you would have found design studios, engineering departments and workshops heaving with activity – without a Mini in sight.

This, don't forget, was the period when the Rover Group was moving closer and closer to Honda, and much of its technical engineering effort was already based on Honda models. In one area you might have seen the new 600s and the re-skinned 800s, in another you might have seen early examples of new-generation 200s and 400s – and there would also be early prototypes of an exciting new mid-engined sports car, the MGF.

But no Minis. The Rover Group, which British Aerospace had owned since 1988, no longer had much interest in the Mini. Sales of the existing models had slumped, and the planners could see no economic way of producing a new model. Not only that, but they would not consider producing new engine derivatives, or any other mechanical derivative involving big capital expenditure.

Rover's policy towards the Mini – if a 'do nothing' approach could be called a policy – was that, quite simply, it would carry on in production as long as people wanted to buy the current models, and as long as that specification could meet the legislation in the countries which took most Mini production.

Company spokesmen were always diplomatic, and sometimes professionally evasive, but their consistent message was always the same: 'Just so long as it's "legal", we'll keep making the Mini, but after that ...'

Since the Mini – the 'Classic' Mini, the 'dear old Mini' as many were now calling it – now sold strongly only in Britain and Japan, it was easy enough to keep up with that policy, especially as a constant stream of special editions kept the little car in the headlines.

Swimming against the tide

That might have been the official line, but all over the company, it seems, there were product planners who wanted to get rid of the car completely. Chris Lee, who would later direct the new MINI engineering programme, once told me that: 'It became quite amusing to see just how many people there were who had drawn up a product plan showing the demise of Mini. And then when it got there, no-one had the courage actually to go through with it ...'

Lined up against them, there was always a small group of *refuseniks* who thought it high time that something *was* done! Fred Coultas, who had been project director on the early Mini Metro model, quipped that: 'Some of us have been trying to replace the Mini since about 1964!'

There always seemed to be people who would find the corner of a workshop (and some other project's budget!) to fiddle about with the layout – maybe a Metro-

Although the second-generation Rover 200 was announced after BMW had bought Rover, the German management always treated it with disdain. 'Not invented here', they implied.

The second generation Rover 200 was a smart little hatchback, and Longbridge's best seller. Its engine was the excellent K-series, but this would prove to be too large to fit into a new MINI.

style Hydragas version here, a conventional coil spring version there, a car with a front-mounted radiator, or one with a new type of hatchback. Dr Alex Moulton, whose Moulton Developments company had evolved all three high-tech, suspension systems – rubber cones, Hydrolastic and Hydragas – was always enthusiastic. This, though, was all unofficial, and inevitably came to nothing.

'We'd always thought that the Mini was very interesting,' Chris Lee recalls,' but we'd never really had our eyes opened to what a powerful brand it actually was ... we'd tended to think of Mini only as a product name, not as a brand name.' A brand, incidentally, which was rapidly fading away before the creators' very eyes.

Even so, the newly founded Advanced Vehicle Engineering organisation, which was being run at Gaydon by Nick Stephenson, was constantly dabbling with

Minis, if only on paper, or in cut-and-shut exercises. Nothing serious, you understand, nothing official or according to any product plan, but there, nevertheless.

Not that Rover's current owners, British Aerospace, seemed to care very much. With only a short-term view of running the business, they seemed to spend as much time 'rationalising' it – which meant closing factories and redeveloping the sites – as they did building it up.

Cowley (or Oxford, as BMW now likes everyone to call it) was a case in point. Before 1992 this sprawling site, originally a combination of Morris Motors and Pressed Steel Co. Ltd, had been integrated by British Leyland (later Rover) but was still really three separate plants, bisected by main roads, and interlinked by overhead conveyors to carry body shells.

In mid-1990, BAe announced that it was to downsize the complex, to spend a

fortune on converting the old 'Pressed Steel' factory (or 'Cowley East' as it become known) and to close down the existing Cowley North and Cowley South plants. Assembly of existing Maestro, Montego and original-Rover 800 types was run down, after which (1992/1993) the re-skinned 800 and the brand-new 600 were put into production at Cowley East/'Oxford'.

Soon after this, BAe's property development arm, Arlington Securities, saw that the historic buildings were speedily razed to the ground and, in short order, two new 'Industrial Parks' took their place. No trace of Cowley North or Cowley South now remains.

BAe, in the meantime, was in financial trouble, which had been caused by catastrophic losses in its civil aircraft division, and it needed to cut back its business diversity. Concluding that although running a car-making business was good for raising cash, it was different from making ultra-costly aircraft, especially from providing wings for the Airbus project.

Accordingly, it was already planning to

sell off Rover Group. Having paid a mere £150 million to the British Government in 1988 to take the ailing business off the hands of the state (with an agreement that it would not then try to dispose of the business for at least five years), it had received approaches from several concerns.

Honda was prepared to increase its shareholding (but only to 47.5 per cent), while BMW was prepared to pay £800 million in cash. Group chairman, George Simpson, would have preferred to sell out to Honda, with whom Rover group and its ancestors had been linked since 1979, but the BMW offer – of a straight purchase – was irresistible.

Negotiated through the winter of 1993/1994, the deal finally went public in February 1994, and became official in March 1994. Within hours, Bernd Pischetsrieder took over as Rover Group's new chairman and, along with his Research & Development chief Wolfgang Reitzle, immediately took control.

BMW straight away guaranteed that they would invest a lot more in new-model development than BAe had ever managed – promising to spend at least £450 million

Early in the 1990s, and before they bought Rover, BMW considered making electric-powered small cars to meet proposed Californian legislation. These thoughts then progressed to the idea of having a 'hybrid' machine – one with an 85bhp water-cooled motorcycle type petrol engine up front, and 45bhp electric motors and batteries in the tail. This was the final derivative of E1, revealed in September 1993, which showed the way that the Munich Design Centre's thinking was moving on small cars. Note that the BMW spinner and kidney grille is still much in evidence.

Another approach to BMW small-car motoring came in March 1993, when the company showed the Z13 project car, a compact and fascinating city-car with a rear-mounted four-cylinder BMW motorcycle engine in the tail, and with only three-seats – the driving seat being in the centre of the car. Just for fun, maybe, but once again it showed how the Design Studio's thoughts were moving at that time.

every year instead of £200 million. Much of that money, they told Rover's management, would be allocated to the Mini.

BMW, it seems, had identified the Mini as a priceless brand – a brand to be rated at the same level as 'Coca Cola', 'McDonalds' and 'Nike' – and they were determined to revive it.

'When they asked us about the Mini,' Chris Lee says, 'they were pretty horrified when we said that: "When we can't keep it legal, we're going to let it run down."'

'We told BMW that we had never been able to make a business case for doing a new Mini – that the margins always looked tiny, and that we needed to make a lot of them to get all the scale benefits.

'BMW immediately said : "We are prepared to fund an all-new small-car platform, in fact we've been working on our schemes for a number of years, in front-wheel-drive. We have configured it, and we think it would work as a Mini".'

BMW, in fact, had taken a different view of the Mini from the day that they took control of the business: 'When we had discussions with colleagues from Rover,' Torsten Muller-Oetvoes recalls, 'we said we wanted to make a success of Mini, they all said: "Why? Forget it …" – they were not really very interested in this little jewel. And it *is* a jewel – one which just needed to be polished up once again.

'No-one at Rover appeared to have a feeling for how valuable the Mini brand could be for them. There was no emotion there – emotion is a key essential for getting premium prices. You are only ready to pay the price if you get that certain gut feeling – I Want This Car. And that's the big difference, say, between a VW Polo and a Mini.'

That was one breakthrough. The other was that if BMW decided to sell a new Mini through BMW dealerships (or alongside them …) then it would open up a far greater number of outlets on a

34

global basis, *including the USA*. The emphasis on the Mini as a brand, a stand-alone motor car, was already enshrined in BMW's strategy for Rover Group, not least because, by definition, it would need to have a completely different layout from all existing, and planned, BMWs.

The Mini, by definition, was the archetypal front-wheel-drive car, and to consider any other layout for a new-generation car would be unthinkable. Yet this ran contrary to BMW's way of designing cars. Extensive, not to say acrimonious, debate at Munich had already settled one thing – that no future BMW would have front-wheel-drive.

Yet the company had often studied the layout – at the same time as it looked at the opportunities of building rear-engined cars – and it had already done much work on

small 'city' cars with such installations. Accordingly, the packaging of front-wheel-drive, and the challenge of producing smart little four-seaters, was already understood. Such work sometimes allowed prototypes, show cars and concept cars to be built with such systems.

In the early 1990s, the threat of North American legislation which would require all car makers to develop zero-emissions models caused the study of electric-powered machines. First shown in 1991, the E1 was a cute and stubby little four-seater, with a typical BMW-style nose, and with an electric power pack (and 44bhp electric motor) in the tail.

This was never meant to be a production car – with a light aluminium frame, with a battery pack costed at £17,000 and with drum brakes it could never be that – but it was, at least, an intriguing 'think piece'.

Minki Two was a remarkable project car, dreamed up in 1994 by the Rover Advanced Vehicle Engineering department. Two inches wider, and two inches longer than the standard Mini, it somehow housed a 16-valve K-Series engine and five-speed gearbox under the bonnet. Hydragas suspension, of Metro/Rover 100 type, was also a feature. (David Wigmore/MINI MAGAZINE)

A famous
false start
– the 9X

The new MINI which finally went on sale in 2001 was one of many projects which had been intended to take over from the original. In the 1960s, 1970s *and* 1980s several new projects had been set up, though all these

schemes had foundered. The first, and most significant, was 9X, an even tinier machine than the 1959-generation Mini, which Alec Issigonis conceived in 1967 when the original car was still at the height of its fame.

Like the original, 9X had a transverse engine, front-wheel-drive and was carefully packaged, but had nothing in common with the existing car. Not only was it several inches *shorter* than the already-tiny Mini, but it was lighter, had a new overhead-camshaft

engine and a crisply-shaped hatchback body style. It was more space-efficient, more economical and would have enjoyed better performance.

Completed soon after the British Leyland merger took place, the only prototype took to the road at exactly the wrong time. British Leyland's management could not see any way of financing this all-new car, and cancelled the project. One prototype still survives – in the BMIHT collection at Gaydon.

When BMW came to engineer the new MINI, everyone insisted that the Rover K-Series engine was too wide to fit. Yet in Minki Two, which was only two inches wider than a standard Classic Mini, it slipped snugly into place. Funny, that …
(David Wigmore/MINI MAGAZINE)

The top speed, BMW claimed, was 75mph, but as 0–50mph would take 18.0 seconds (BMW never even dared to estimate a 0–60mph time!), this one was all-set to become another traffic-jam-causing snail.

E2, which followed early in 1992, was a longer-wheelbase development of E1, with a more powerful, 55bhp, electric package, a bigger cabin and with an estate-car type of tail – but once again this was no more than a research project.

E1 was eventually written off in a fire, a conflagration which started in its own propulsion systems, but in the meantime BMW also produced the Z13 project,

another aluminium-framed city-sized car in the same mould (this time it was 135in/3440mm long). Revealed in March 1993, this was another compact little rear-engined, two-door, three-seater machine, with sharply-detailed styling and vast 16in wheels. And this time it was a real performance car, for power was by an 85bhp/1,100cc water-cooled four-cylinder engine which had been lifted straight out of the existing BMW K1100RS motorcycle, which drove through a CVT automatic transmission.

Practical? Certainly – for even though the seating package gave only a centrally-placed front-seat for the driver, with rear passengers behind and to each side of him, here was a car with a claimed 112mph top speed and BMW-standard handling, and interior trim and equipment to match – but it never made it beyond the one-off stage. BMW's directors, it seems, were not convinced that such a machine was right for BMW's perceived image (too small, too dumpy, too down-market?), and the project was cancelled.

One further attempt was then made to break through into credibility. In September 1993, the final E1 project car appeared, with styling related to the Z13, with another variation and update on the aluminium structure concept – but this time with a petrol engine/electric power hybrid power installation.

Early design studies for a new MINI were all evolutionary, and envisaged how the original might have changed over the years. The nose in this early sketch already shows off the cowled headlamps which are a feature of the production car.

Still a four-seater, still styled and badged as a BMW – effectively this could have become the company's 'city car' to meet still-pending Californian zero-emissions regulations – the 1993 E1 was an ambitious machine, which placed its 82bhp K1100 motorcycle engine and CVT automatic transmission up front, where it drove the front wheels, and a 45bhp electric motor and a massive rechargeable battery pack in the tail, driving the rear wheels.

Although the two drive systems could not be used together, computer control allowed spare 'petrol' power, regenerated under braking, to be fed into the electrical batteries – yet those batteries still needed overnight recharging to get them back into peak condition. This, though, was yet another concept car that went almost straight from the press launch to obscurity – and it never went on sale.

First thoughts

When BMW bought Rover Group in 1994, this was not the only work they had done in Germany on small cars. Extensive research into front-wheel-drive had already

been conducted, as had structural and packaging work on small four-seaters. A larger front-wheel-drive model, incidentally, had also been investigated, and it was from those schemes that the Rover 75 (which was finally launched in 1998) was finally evolved.

And as Dr Heinrich Petra, who was the original project leader on what BMW called their E50 project (the new MINI) in 1995 and later headed the MINI project team from 2000, also reminded me: 'We had a lot of activity in the front-wheel-drive area – a lot of prototype experience, we knew what we wanted to achieve. Plus 4x4 activity – 3-Series, for instance – because in principle that was the same set of problems at the front of the car.'

Once Bernd Pischetsrieder had made it clear that BMW wanted to revive the Mini, British design staff were instantly encouraged to start looking at new schemes. At this stage, though, they were not to know (BMW management quite deliberately kept the two teams apart) that BMW was also forging ahead with its own ideas.

Such a two-pronged approach would no doubt be considered wasteful by other car-makers, but even today BMW is not repentant. Already highly profitable, it wanted to stay that way, by expanding down market (to the Mini sector) – and eventually up-market by the purchase of the Rolls-Royce brand.

Rover was also pleased that Pischetsrieder already seemed to understand the enormous emotional appeal of the Mini. To observers, even though there was no way that a new model could be put on sale within four or five years, it certainly seemed to be one of his pet projects. When questions were raised about the eventual assembly site for a new car, he stated that: 'The Mini is *the* British motor car, so where else on earth should it be built but at Longbridge? The factory is so much part of the Mini's identity. At Longbridge you find people who have spent their entire working life helping to build the Mini.'

Certainly Longbridge needed a new model to flesh out its huge and under-used

assembly sheds, for in 1994 output there was running at only about two-thirds of its 450,000 cars/year capacity.

For the first time since the 1970s, therefore, Rover Group themselves began serious work on a new Mini-car, this finally putting the future of the existing Mini in doubt. The first conclusion, which was resisted only by a few diehards, was that any all-new model, no question, would have to be a lot larger than before. Since 1959 the world had changed, people had got larger, more comfort and space were demanded, modern crash test and safety regulations had proliferated, these all inevitably pointing towards the use of a bigger, heavier and much more solid structure.

Even while the design studios, led by Geoff Upex, and with Dave Saddington looking after Mini projects, were beginning to develop truly radical proposals, there was time for one act of defiance on the theme of the old model. With no Product Planning input, with virtually no budget

Designers in Munich, led by Frank Stephenson, soon homed in on this E50 MINI theme, complete with large wheels, cowled headlamps, a straight-through waistline, and an essentially flat roof.

and with the effort confined to the Advanced Vehicle Engineering department, Tony Spillane's small team speedily built two one-off prototypes which they christened Minki One and Minki Two.

Minki Two, a prototype which has survived and is housed in the BMIHT collection at the Heritage Centre, had one simple purpose – to see how far an existing Mini needed to be changed for a modern K-Series engine and end-on five-speed gearbox to be installed, and for Metro/Rover 100-type Hydragas suspension to be used. (Minki One, on the other hand, took the more radical step of inserting a three-cylinder version of the K-Series engine into an unmodified body shell – this three-cylinder engine figures again in the story, in Spiritual, which I describe later in this chapter).

The result was a smartly-detailed and furnished car, looking like a Mini except for being subtly and by no means obviously a little bulkier: 'They did a "hot-cross-bun" job on it,' Chris Lee recalls, 'by carving it

wider and longer, then welding it up again. It still looked like an old Mini.'

Although the 75bhp 16-valve 1.4-litre K-Series engine and its five-speed gearbox were larger than the ancient Mini-type A-Series engine which had been discarded, once the car's overall width had been increased by a mere 2.0in/50mm, the new assembly slotted neatly into place. The car was also just 2.0in/50mm longer than before, and with Rover 100-style 13in cast alloy wheels it looked very smart. Chris Lee remembers it with affection: 'It was an interesting experience to drive, basically a Mini with Mini characteristics, but brought up to date, and with a modern engine and transmission … But as a new model, it didn't mean anything, because a new car wouldn't have looked like that.'

Even so, this was more of a 'Told you we could do it …', rather than a 'Why don't we …?' exercise, for it simply could not offer the level of crash test performance, nor the driving position, nor the refinement it would have wanted.

Right from the start, there was no argument about the MINI's *general shape, which would include a full-depth hatchback.*

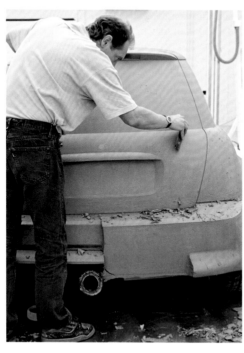

The E50 Mini full-size clay model taking shape. Clearly this was going to be a much larger car than the Classic Mini which it would replace.

In 1995 and 1996, when the E50 Mini's exterior theme was taking shape, the Munich design team was led by Frank Stephenson.

Which explains, no doubt, why Minki Two was handed over for display in the Heritage Centre a full two years before the Mini actually went on sale.

Serious studies

In the meantime, serious concept work on a new small car was getting under way. Rover's project work, centred on the new Design Centre at Gaydon, got going under Geoff Upex and Dave Saddington while, unbeknown to them, BMW's project team also began to beaver away in Munich. As both teams were eventually to discover, Rover's ideas were much more radical than those being dreamed up in Germany.

Both, however, had already been told that such a new car would be a Mini – and not a BMW. The new car, no matter whether ultra-small or ultra-high-tech, would be a brand on its own.

'Although BMW was always thinking around the idea of doing a small BMW,' Torsten Muller-Oetvoes, Mini Brand Director and Product Manager commented, 'They definitely did not concern a small car like a Mini. Then with Rover, we found we had the Mini, as another brand. Mini is the most emotional, and the most high-impact brand in the small sector.'

BMW, he insisted, would never have put a BMW-badged car of this size and type on sale: 'Definitely not. What BMW stands for is authenticity in all its brands. We could only do a car like this when we had bought the Mini brand. We see Mini as an important tool, to gain new customers. Some people might say that "BMW is very nice, but it's not exactly the car for me. I'm looking for different things in life" – and maybe for those people the Mini is the right target ...'

From the very day that Bernd Pischetsrieder and BAe's Sir Richard Evans shook hands on the deal in 1994, in front of the unmistakable backdrop of the British Houses of Parliament, Rover designers were enthused at the prospect of developing a successor to the Mini. BMW had already made it clear that no new MINI could be ready before 1998/1999, but in Design terms this meant that the project had to begin right away.

Even as early as 1994, designers on both sides of the channel dusted off their sketches of Mini-sized cars and started turning them into models, both scale and full size. Though neither knew that the other was running rival projects, Dave Saddington looked after MINI work at Gaydon, while Frank Stephenson (an American citizen with much experience at GM and Ford before he joined BMW in 1991) forged ahead in Munich.

Even so, it was not until an absolutely seminal date – Tuesday, 17 October 1995 – that the two teams faced each other, when their respective offerings were shown to BMW's directors at a presentation and viewing at a top-secret meeting in the BMIHT Heritage Centre at Gaydon.

Now, incidentally, it can be told. Those of us who wondered why the Rover design staff looked rather breathless when they launched the new Rover 200 at the London Motor Show that afternoon, now know it was because they had been doing even more important things in Warwickshire during the morning, then driven down, helter-skelter, to be in London later in the day.

Knowing that the integrity of the Mini brand had to be preserved at all costs, both teams – British and German – had thought in terms of evolution. After 1959 the Mini, as a style, had not advanced at all, so several 'might have been' re-generations had never taken place.

Both teams, therefore, tried to think along the same lines. What might have happened, how might it have happened and what should a fourth or fifth generation Mini look like?

As Gert Hildebrand, Head of Design, MINI from 2000, confirmed: 'In 40 years

During 1995, Rover's design team evolved this intriguing pair of projects – Spiritual (nearer the camera) and Spiritual Too. Both would have shared the same basic platform, with a mid-rear engine mounted under the rear seating position. Spiritual was a tiny car, only 120in long, and Rover thought it could be the right replacement for the Mini. BMW disagreed.

we have missed out three or four intermediate versions. So we tried to think how those "missing" cars might have turned out …'

Spiritual

What became the 'Evolutionary' themes were consistently similar – for all were meant to have conventional pressed-steel body shells, three-door hatchback styles, transverse engines and front-wheel-drive – but Geoff Upex's British Design Centre, with Dave Saddington running the design team, had another card to play. Putting aside every one of the Mini's existing

styling 'cues' (which every single one of the competing examples from BMW had retained), Rover Group elected to go for something revolutionary in style. A project, eventually known as 'Spiritual', therefore emerged to a modern brief – with modern crash test and safety requirements in mind. How could four people be accommodated in a ten foot length? What would happen if road congestion got worse ? What if fuel prices went through the roof? What can we do to meet these problems?

At this time the engineering project leader, Tim Leverton (he later became involved in the BMW-financed new-Rolls-

ACV30 appeared in 1997 as a Mini motorsport theme car, but was based on the most extreme MINI style proposal which BMW had prepared in 1995. Several basic cues would be carried over to the new-generation MINI.

Royce project) was an enthusiastic 'Revolutionary', and backed Design's packaging ideas to the hilt.

Spiritual, as presented to the BMW board, was a Brave New World in Mini design, for one very good reason – that it carried its engine under the rear seats, and drove the rear wheels. That engine, as projected, but never actually built, was to be a 60bhp, 800cc, three-cylinder version of the single-overhead-camshaft K-Series engine, and an all-new transaxle would have been needed.

Because this was still a very short car – even though it was arranged to have enough front-end 'crush' space to meet all

known, and proposed, crash-test regulations – it was still only 120in/3048mm long – exactly the same as that of the classic Mini.

Not only that, but both Design and Engineering saw Spiritual as the first of a new 'platform' range, and took the opportunity to evolve a larger derivative of this car.

Called Spiritual Too, it kept the same basic central/rear-engine layout, but extended the wheelbase, the platform and the front axle forward. With five doors instead of three, and with a four-cylinder engine instead of three cylinders, it had a

ACV30, as seen in public, used a mid-MGF-engined power train, but its style theme was a 1995 proposal for a new MINI coupé.

much larger interior package (bigger than the new Rover 75, I was told), and was 18in/450mm longer, at 138in/3500mm.

Different cultures then clashed in a hilarious way. Apparently when these project twins were first shown to the Germans, Rover suggested that if the smaller car was to be a Mini, then the larger version should be a Midi. The Germans, not perhaps realising what they were saying, said: 'No, not "Midi" – it needs to be "Maxi" ...' – and they could not understand why the British all collapsed with mirth, and took some time to regain their composure. 'Maxi', you see, was the name of a particularly awful Austin model which British Leyland had made throughout the 1970s.

Design was excited about the prospects for this project, not only because it was a novel solution to many design problems, but because: 'There was plenty of free crush space at the front, we'd got a lot of costings, and weight studies done, a lot of the detail packaging was worked out – all in all it was well thought through.'

At the time, Rover Group found the conclusions of this presentation to be confusing – at least, to them. Leaving the meeting with the impression that their offerings had been preferred over the massed ranks of MINI offerings from BMW, they were soon cast down when it became clear that BMW's designers thought they, too, had been chosen to take their own projects a stage further.

This meant, effectively, that the British designers then wasted much of the winter of 1995/1996 working on further refinement of the Spiritual concept. When Rover Group's marketing staff realised that control of this project was slipping away from then, they were so distressed that they worked up, and issued, an internal document criticising what the Munich studios were offering instead.

The German E50, they suggested, had been styled first, and packaged second, was not thought to be an 'Issigonis way' of doing things, was thought to be 'only better than average', and that it: 'doesn't truly shock with innovation.'

This was ACV30, shown in 1997 to commemorate the 30th Anniversary of three Mini Monte Carlo Rally victories. In some ways its basic proportions would evolve into the new MINI.

The most searing criticism of E50 was that it was '… too serious to have a sense of humour, too slow to be exciting, too average a concept'.

E50 was also thought to be too large – original proposals for an estate car/ 'Traveller' derivative put it at 157in/ 4000mm long ('definitely in the low-medium market sector'), and potentially too expensive. It was likely to be much more costly to make than Spiritual. At this time (late 1995) the estimate was that Spiritual would have sold for £8,500–£10,000, whereas BMW's E50 could not be sold for less than £10,500–£12,500. These latter estimates, in fact, proved to be remarkably accurate, even at 2001 prices.

Although presented for study in a businesslike manner, all the signs are that this critique infuriated BMW's top team, and made it almost inevitable that Spiritual would be binned in short order. And so it was. No running car was ever made, though the mock-ups were preserved.

Spiritual and Spiritual Too, however, were found to be valuable in 1997 when BMW's first controlled leaks were made concerning a new-generation MINI. Dug out of store, tidied up, and made to look like more complete cars, they were revealed at the Geneva Motor Show, where they were received with great interest.

These two cars were described breathlessly, and reverently, by the motoring magazines of the day, as if they were true ancestors of a still-secret 'new MINI', and as if they were pointing the way to an exciting future. But they were not. These mock-ups never even looked like getting the go-ahead, and were tucked away in a storeroom soon afterwards. At the time of writing, they have not been seen since.

ACV30 – a red herring

Even before Spiritual and Spiritual Too were shown, enthusiasts who should have known better were getting very excited when Rover Group showed the ACV30,

immediately before the 1997 Monte Carlo rally. Was this to be the shape of the new MINI, they asked? The truth, though, was more mundane – that this was no more than a variation on a styling theme and, like Spiritual, it had been dreamed up in 1995, then sidelined.

The shape of ACV30, however, was much closer to home than Spiritual had ever been – and I think that many Mini

This was the interior of ACV30, as seen in 1997. Although designers insist that the two themes were separately developed, there are some distinct similarities to the MINI production car layout.

ACV30 drove around the Monaco GP circuit at the 1997 Monte Carlo Rally, ahead of the three 1960s-Monte-winning cars. The publicity gained by this short exercise was priceless.

enthusiasts realised this. Even though it was decked out as a rally car in January 1997, its shape certainly nodded to the proportions of the old Mini in several respects. Since the new MINI has been launched, normally tight-lipped designers have now admitted that the shape, but not the mechanical layout, was one of the various E50 proposals (which I describe in more detail in the next chapter) which were put up at the famous viewing of October 1995: 'That was one of the five BMW designs that was there in October 1995. At the time it was just one of the cars that was supposed to share this front-engined/front-wheel-drive package …'

Like the Spiritual concepts, this was

another of the offerings which became redundant in the winter of 1995/1996. However, for 1997 BMW then decided to make a fuss about the thirtieth anniversary of the Mini's last Monte Carlo Rally victory (this was in January 1967, when Rauno Aaltonen drove a 1275S), and elected to build a running concept car which they would name ACV30. The '30' is obvious, and ACV stood for 'Anniversary Concept Vehicle'.

'ACV30 is designed to encapsulate the spirit of Mini past,' Rover Group's publicity machine insisted, 'in a contemporary style, with detailing representative of future design thinking.'

Under the skin, however, there was an

MGF engine/transmission and rear suspension behind the seats, with MGF front suspension and steering up front, the whole being tied together by a BMW-designed aluminium tubed chassis frame (one of a series, of which E1 and Z13 were family members). The interior was pure late-1990s rally car, with bucket seats and full harness belts.

At a casual glance, the fascia looks to be related to that of the MINI production car but this was apparently not so: 'A lot of people look at the interior of the MINI, and suggest that it is an evolution of what appeared in the ACV30 – but I can tell you that this was pure coincidence. We had all been looking at similarly evolutionary things, had looked at interiors, and reached similar conclusions. The MINI and ACV30 fascias were probably done simultaneously, and certainly independently.

Once again, therefore, BMW and Rover Group reaped much publicity (and, let us be frank, false expectations too) by digging a redundant style out of store and putting it to quite unrelated use. ACV30 certainly made the headlines, in sporting terms it sold the pass, and it showed a way to the future.

That future, by the way, was already taking place behind tight-closed doors in Germany and in the UK. By 1996 work on a brand-new MINI project had been approved.

Soon after the last Classic Mini of all was built in 2000, Nick Stephenson of MG Rover handed it over to Bob Dover (chairman of the BMIHT) for safekeeping at the Gaydon Museum. Those are the BMIHT trustees in the background, along with 'Old Number One'.

3 Engineering the new car

MINI takes shape

Two dates were absolutely pivotal to the evolution of E50 – the new MINI – which went on sale in 2001. One was 17 October 1995, when the first Design confrontation took place between the Germans and the British. The other was 22 May 1996, when BMW's Policy Committee abruptly decided to hand over the entire project to the Rover Group for completion.

This all sounds decisive – and BMW would like the rest of the world to go on believing that it was so – but a great deal of 'fudging and smudging' (to quote one top British engineer) had already taken place along the way. There would be more.

One British designer clearly remembers the 1995 presentation: 'With Spiritual and Spiritual Too, we were ranged against a load of design offerings from BMW design. As the covers came off, what became clear was that whilst we had been framing the debate with some very "stretching" concepts, BMW had produced no fewer than five different models – we had not been working on any of these. They came from far and wide – one of them from BMW's advanced studio in California.

'When we saw their models it became clear that they had already settled on a theme, and were looking at variations on that theme. They were close – gratifyingly close – to the front-engine/front-wheel-drive "Evolution" ideas we had already done. For us, it seemed, this was one possible way of perpetuating the Mini, but for BMW, clearly this was the *only* possible way.'

As I have already noted, there appeared to be no clear conclusion from that meeting. Both camps seemed to think their offerings had received favour (the British, of course, having displayed Spiritual and Spiritual Too), and little was resolved until the early weeks of 1996. At top level, though, BMW seemed to have no doubt – that their Munich-prepared E50 ideas were the best, and that these were to be translated into running motor cars as soon as possible.

Even in the autumn of 1995, the best of the projects presented by BMW was a truly compelling piece of styling design. Completed by American-born Frank Stephenson, it was quite remarkably similar to what today's MINI Cooper has become, but there were two major problems still to be addressed.

Major? Indeed – for there was, as yet, no 'people package' and no 'mechanical package' for the new car. In layman's terms, this meant that BMW was going on the basis of: 'Well, we'll find an engine in due course, and of course we're sure that we can somehow get four people into this seating package …'

Which is not, if the brutal truth be told, the ideal way to start developing an all-new car. The only full-sized model which existed at that time was a beautifully-detailed see-through fibreglass mock-up, which looked like a real car. But no human being, nor even one of BMW's 'dummies', had yet entered it …

There were several practical engineering problems in producing the MINI's bonnet as one massive pressing. Both Rover and BMW Design wanted more curvature, but this proved difficult to press, and the profile had to be eased before the car went on sale.

48

BMW designers always insisted that the MINI should have a comfortable driving position, equally as spacious as that of the BMW 3-series. No 'truck-like' steering wheel position on this car!

BMW, it seems, was not at all perturbed about this. They were so confident in their technical abilities, that these shortcomings were seen only as technical problems which could, and would, be overcome.

The BMW Board, however, had instructed the Munich team to go ahead on the basis of refining the Munich style, but adopting as much as possible of the packaging work which the *British* team had already proposed. This, by the way, is typical of any Board's way of thinking – their job, as they saw it, was to make decisions, while their staff were meant to translate anything they decided into acceptable fact.

Two into one ...

First, though, it was necessary to bring two rather disparate themes together. In October 1995 there had been not one, but two, preferred exterior styles. At this early stage, the Board had already decided to carry on using the 'Cooper' model name for a more sporty and higher-powered version – but with one difference. Way

back in the 1960s, F1 race car constructor John Cooper had inspired the birth of the first Mini-Cooper, then raced many of the succeeding derivatives. This time around, and still as a much-respected Mini-Cooper franchised dealer, tuner and enthusiast, he would merely be consulted about what was proposed – and he would receive a regular reward for the use of his name on the latest cars.

BMW's first intention was to distinguish a car called MINI One from MINI Cooper by the use of different roof lines. One had a conventional roof, but the Cooper had been created as a 2+2 coupé. Space for rear-seat passengers was heavily compromised, so much so that 12-year-olds might have got comfortable there, but no-one older or larger.

Not only did the British team resist the 2+2 layout, but in any case thought it to be an economic non-starter: 'We actually thought that for a limited number of cars,' 1996–1999 project leader Chris Lee commented, 'that it was not feasible to have two roof heights, and we also thought that it was going to be very difficult to sell a "2+2" Cooper, and a four-seater for adults as well. Then there would be different crash tests, and lots of extra investment in body assembly equipment. We thought it was folly.'

Project work, however, went ahead until the spring of 1996, this being centred in Munich, Germany, but with a growing number of British designers and engineers moving temporarily to Munich to add their expertise. To be honest, there was a good deal of friction between the two nationalities, many counter-proposals, and progress was slow, though a couple of fully-styled 'mules' were constructed.

Amazingly, these looked like the proposed styles – one high-roof, one low-roof Cooper type – but were built up on otherwise standard Fiat Punto platforms and running gear. They would be an integral part of the upheaval which was to follow.

Quite suddenly, however, there was an

abrupt change of direction. On 22 May 1996, BMW's Policy Committee met in a day-long meeting at the British Design Studio, where Bernd Pischetsrieder and Wolfgang Reitzle surveyed Rover group's business progress.

'I was called in at the end of the day.' Chris Lee recalls. 'Pischetsrieder told me that: "A decision has been made, Mr Lee. Rover is now to be responsible for the delivery of E50, the new MINI, and as the existing small and sports car platform director, you are to be its leader." I had had no warning. It was a sudden as that.'

There was more. Because BMW's staff was very efficient at explicitly following instructions, by the end of that day – not the end of the week, or the end of the month – all work on E50 in Germany had stopped.

Reporting direct to Rover Group's Nick Stephenson, Chris Lee (whose previous credits included direction of the MGF project) had a mountain to climb: 'This move did create a terrible lull in the programme, with absolutely nobody ready to pick this project up. Some people in BMW did see the sense of putting together "hand-over packages" …

'I had to start from nothing – a clean sheet. I begged and pleaded with Dr Burkhard Goschel [Director of Special Model Series and in charge of E50 development at that time] to continue until I could ramp up the skills and resources, until we could assemble the basic know-how. But no – Goschel merely said: "We are no longer responsible for E50. We have stopped." Dr Goschel made it clear that by the time he stepped off the plane in Munich

When engineering the body shell, Rover and BMW made sure that the passenger doors opened as wide as possible. Not possible, I reckon, in a crowded supermarket parking lot!

Front-
wheel
drive

Don't believe the romantics who will tell you that BMC's Mini was the first important front-wheel-drive car. It was not – for, in fact, several successful front-wheel-drive cars had already been on sale since the 1930s.

Citroën had startled the world with its innovative *Traction Avant* model in 1934, while DKW of Germany put a series of small two-stroke-engined front-drive cars on sale in the 1930s, these DKWs later being used as the inspiration for the first Swedish Saabs of the late 1940s. Then, of course, there was the cheap and cheerful – but incredibly effective – Citroën 2CV, which had been designed just before the outbreak of World War Two, but which eventually went on sale in 1948.

Where Issigonis's original Mini started a new trend was by combining front-wheel drive, a transversely-mounted four-cylinder engine, and ingenious space utilisation in an incredibly small piece of packaging. It was by showing that an otherwise conventional in-line engine could be realigned, and made useful with front-wheel drive, that the original Mini changed the face of late-twentieth-century motoring.

Once the Mini's point had been made, its layout was eventually copied by companies around the world – by Fiat in 1969, by VW in 1974, and by Ford (with the Fiesta) in 1976. Nowadays, the vast majority of all new models have transverse engines and front-wheel drive.

The new MINI, incidentally, was BMW's very first front-wheel-drive production car – which explains, perhaps, one reason why it was not called a BMW, but sold as a brand on its own merits.

that evening, all work on the E50 would already have ceased.

'BMW immediately handed over everything to us – they did an extremely professional and technical handover of everything that they had done so far – so that all the data, all the technical information, all the modelling and digital information, came to us.'

At this point, therefore, E50 became

Like every other modern hatchback, the MINI *had very adaptable rear loading arrangements. On the* MINI *Cooper shown, the rear seat backrest was split, so that half could be folded forward, the other half left erect.*

R50 (R standing for Rover Group, of course). Lee was given no extra time to carry out the transition, and the struggle to keep up with a timetable began in earnest. By this time Job One – the target date for series production to begin – had been fixed for September 2000, when new Longbridge assembly and body-in-white facilities were due to crank into action. That was already one year later than BMW had desired – but they had brought this on themselves by all the in-fighting, the second-guessing and the high-fashion fighting which had gone on so far.

BMW, in the meantime, had already allowed for the introduction of a new MINI at Longbridge, by deciding to kill off the Rover 100 at the end of 1998, and to allow the Classic Mini to potter on towards a natural death in the autumn of 2000.

No partly-engineered motor cars had yet been built – only the pair of cars, based on Fiat Puntos, that Rover rather sweetly describe as 'mules' – there was no chosen engine ready to power the car, and the platform engineering was not finalised. Nor had the design and styling of the car been finalised – neither the exterior nor, especially, the interior which had barely been started.

With deadlines and release dates already beginning to crowd in upon him, Chris Lee had to rush to set up his engineering team at Longbridge. Looking back over the years, he recalls how awful it was in the first weeks, because the resources were simply not in place. Over time, in fact, BMW made sure that there would never be any operating budget problems, but it was the sheer lack of people which frustrated progress for a time.

Brian Griffin, who was currently running the MGF engineering programme, was one of the first to be tapped – he immediately took charge of Vehicle Engineering – and, like Lee, he then had to 'steal' people from other on-going projects to fill out the project.

At least nine months were lost, he reckons, by this totally unplanned, and

Frank Stephenson (right) was the leader of the design team which shaped the original E50 MINI exterior style studies. Here he and a colleague are studying proposals for the door trims of the new car.

When you park a new MINI alongside a classic example, you soon see how much larger it has become. This dimensioned drawing makes this very clear. The new MINI is longer, wider, heavier – in fact, more substantial in every feature.

abrupt, change of responsibility from Munich to the UK. There was an added problem. At this time the Rover Group (for which read BMW, of course) was in the throes of relocating and centralising all its engineering and design staff to a brand-new building at the test track at Gaydon – some from Longbridge, some from the last remaining Triumph buildings at Canley and some from the Land Rover factory at Solihull. Work on the new MINI, therefore, began at Canley, Gaydon and Longbridge,

and would not be finally settled at Gaydon for months to come.

While Lee got on with project direction, the absorption of data and other information from Munich and liaison with Design, Griffin and his new team started detail work on the chassis and running gear: 'In June 1996, when we started, there was already a set of targets which defined what the car was supposed to be. The delivery of those targets hadn't been sorted at all – not how we were going to get the turning circle, not how we were going to package the suspension, not how we were to fit an engine and transmission into place, not how we were going to get a practical crash structure – none of that had been settled.

'The design had certainly been done, but the delivery of it wasn't anywhere. At that moment, too, the likely cost of the car was massively over target, though when BMW handed it over they claimed that they had a strategy planned to get back to the cost. But they hadn't!

'The programme gradually lengthened so that we were struggling to meet a late-2000 Job One schedule. Even so, it was always a tight programme. All the budgets had been settled the previous November … There were some Rover people who had already been over in Munich, doing concept work, and those people carried on working for us, so that helped.'

BMW, who to this day insist that all the concept work had been completed in Munich and that only detail work was henceforth needed in the UK, soon found themselves sending engineers, designers and staff to the UK on a regular basis.

'We supported them from Munich,' says Dr Petra. 'We met with them every week, sometimes two times a week.'

Maybe this transport flow was not as intense, or as large, as that carried out regularly by Ford (who actually have a small airline, FordAir, for the purpose), but there were regular charter flights between Munich and the UK. Many Germans became very familiar with Birmingham's

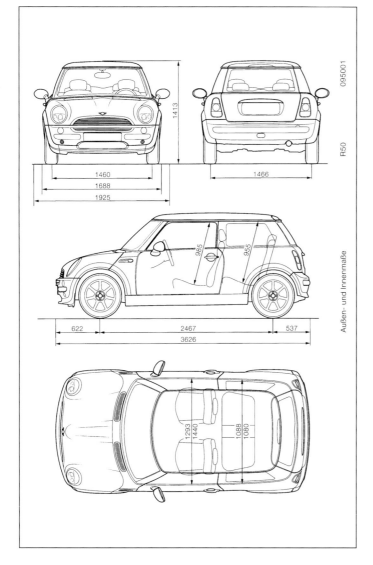

1959-2000

airport, and with the 30 mile dash up and down the M42 and M40 motorways which connected it to the new Group Technical Centre at Gaydon, south of Warwick. Catering staff at Gaydon learned to prepare European, rather than purely British, food.

The flow of faces and expertise was massive, and two-way, but somehow rarely friendly. BMW, it seemed, had already decided that Rover Group, as an operation, was less capable than they had originally hoped, and the master-servant aura gradually increased. It did not bode well for the future. In 1999 it came to a head – and in 2000 it would end in an acrimonious split.

In the meantime, the design team at Gaydon (which had never really lost touch with the developing E50 project since late 1995) was beginning to take shape. Rover's Geoff Upex (who was already finalising the new Rover 75) was to be in overall control, while Dave Saddington became Design

Manager. It was Dave who had the job of taking Stephenson's original exterior styles, rationalising them into one shape (for the two-body strategy had finally been cancelled, much to everyone's relief), finalising them, making them what the industry calls 'feasible' for manufacture, inspiring the birth of an interior – and releasing them all on time to meet that Job One date, which was looking increasingly ambitious with every passing day.

Upex and Saddington then had to set up close links with Chris Lee, who soon appointed Brian Griffin as his chassis engineering chief. All through Rover Group, the news of these appointments was greeted with real satisfaction, as all were renowned 'can-do' exponents. (And so they should have been – for Lee's father had been a long-time manager at Triumph, later British Leyland, while Griffin's father, Charles, was for a long time Alec Issigonis's right-hand-man and lynch-pin, and later

Throughout 1995 and 1996, BMW and their associates at Rover battled to keep many design 'cues', or character elements, of the old Mini, in the shape of the new MINI. Look carefully at this, the last of the old-type cars, and you will see from details such as the smiley-front face, round headlamps, horizontal grille and brightwork, wheel styles, wheelarch extensions and the angle of the windscreen and the waist plus roof lines that this was achieved.

became Technical Director.) Even while Lee's growing team (experts were begged, poached and borrowed from other projects, simply to get the R50 show on the road!) was coming together, Design's first achievement was to make sense of the styling.

'The biggest task that we were faced with,' says one experienced designer, 'was that we were originally meant to deliver two completely different bodies, with two different roof heights.'

Yet, all that was handed over to them from BMW in May 1996 was one clay model which had been seen at the October 1995 presentation, the two Punto-based 'mules' which were only visually correct as far as skin lines and panels were concerned, and a mountain of sketches, computer models and other data.

This clay was the low-roofed Stephenson creation which had won the 'beauty

contest' but which could only ever be a 2+2-seater. At the same time BMW still thought that there was to be the high-roof option, which looked very ungainly ('way too tall'), rather like some awkwardly-detailed Japanese small cars which were appearing at that time.

Wolfgang Reitzle's decision to have the 'mules' made at an early stage was important, for he believed that a new shape should not only be seen in a studio, and in a secure viewing garden, but also on the road. What would it look like from behind, from the side, in the rear-view mirror of another car, on the autobahn, or in a city street? The very existence of these 'mules' hastened the big decision in July 1996: 'Finally we had a gathering at BMW's test track at Miramar in France,' Lee told me, 'where we were finally able to convince everyone that only a single body style made sense. We gave them theoretical and

All Minis, Gert Hildebrand says, should have horizontal waistlines, a roof gutter line to match and, of course, they needed a wheel at each corner. The new Mini had all such features.

practical reasons – and it was at the viewing, outside in the fresh air, that they all saw the high-roof version. To them, it had started to look far less like a Mini, and rather more Japanese, like a Nissan Micra. This was anathema to BMW.'

Saddington's brief – to finalise one acceptable style, which would at once look sporty, have all the flavour of an 'evolution' Mini and be able to carry four adults – was triumphantly achieved well before the end of 1996. Not that there ever seemed to be enough time – by almost any industry standards this was to be a very rapid programme indeed – but the shape which settled down at that point was the one which went on sale in 2001, and is so distinctive.

The result was a car with that instantly recognisable nose (though it isn't quite so sloping as you might think – have a look from the side to see the subtle swelling over

the radiator core), with a number of original Classic Mini styling cues retained intact – and a car which was much larger, overall, than many pundits were expecting. There were several reasons for this.

Dr Heinrich Petra (Head of the MINI project team from 1999): 'First of all, the new car had to reach the NCAP 4-star crash test rating. The world's customers expect this. When we try to achieve this with the MINI, we need so much length in front of the cabin, the bulkhead. We need enough crush length. In fact these days you have to crash test the car from the front, from the side, and from the front-offset as well. The European tests are just as severe as the American tests.

'Secondly, with BMW an important factor in any "driver's" car is the driving position. So the MINI had to have the same driving position as a 3-Series. On the new MINI, what we call the "H-Point" [the

One important new design detail of the MINI was that the angle of the screen was replicated in the panel gap/joint at the rear of the lift-up bonnet assembly. Think of the exposed panel seam on old-type Minis …

The finalised design for the new MINI Cooper featured a smiley-type grille with much brightwork, and cast alloy wheels to emphasise the sporty character of the car. This 2001/2002 model emphasises the squat stance of the new chassis.

position of the driver's hip joint] in relation to the pedals was therefore fixed. On the old Mini, well, the driving position was like a lorry …

'Big wheels, too, help from the comfort point of view. On this car it is possible to have 17in wheels. Then, of course, you have to have space for the passengers! Really, we could not make the MINI any smaller and still achieve all the standards, and all the conditions…'

The point has been made, repeatedly, that the MINI driver sits low down, and central to the steering wheel and pedals – as in the BMW 3-Series. In the old Mini, not only was the steering wheel much more horizontal than would be acceptable today,

but it was not in line with the chassis of the car, nor were the pedal positions.

Chris Lee: 'It grew because it had to. Primarily, this was to do with keeping a conventional layout – a transverse engine and end-on gearbox, mounted upright, plus all the ancillaries. Then, with all that equipment under the bonnet, it was all about getting the right crash test performance. The major challenge was trying to find a crash performance, a crush mechanism, that was going to do the job. We had to try to get good crush beams, good longitudinals, in there, but they took up a lot of space.

'In the list of targets we had to agree with the BMW Board, one was that we had to have a turning circle of not more than 33ft/10 metres. With that, and with the need to package up to 18in wheels, you can see the size of the wheelarch envelope we needed.

'The wheels, too, were big – and that was a Reitzle obsession. On the new MINI, he wanted to make the wheels a dominant feature: on the Classic Mini, he always reminded us that the last cars had 12in, or even 13in wheels, so to use 16in wheels on the new car was in proportion.

'If all the talked-about derivatives appear, then I believe we will see 18in or even 19in wheels on the tuned versions.'

Torsten Muller-Oetvoes: 'Of course the new car is bigger than the Classic Mini, but that is because of the safety regulations and related items. Yet all the genes, the DNA, of the original Mini have been preserved.'

Gert Hildebrand (Head of Design, MINI from 2000): In the last 40 years, the average size of people has grown by at least 4in/100mm. Plus, you have to have space for all the safety features – crash tests, air bags, air-conditioning, driving comfort – all these things.'

In 2001 terms, therefore, these were all persuasive and compelling arguments. And the finalised car could have been even larger. At one stage the engineers asked for an extra 4in/100mm in length – a longer front overhang – to ease the crash test

performance, but the styling designers held their ground and refused: A Mini, they said, *has* to have a wheel at each corner to look right.

One Rover Group company insider, who refuses to be named in this case, put it succinctly: 'It certainly isn't an Issigonis package. Basically what BMW did was to take something approaching a VW Golf driving package, which may not be too different from the BMW 3-Series, and designed a Mini round it. What you've ended up with is really a 2+2, it really doesn't have any rear leg-room. It has a very straight-legged driving position, the very antithesis of what Sir Alec would have done ...'

Ideally, the engineers would have liked something like 19.7in/500mm of 'free crush space' in which to absorb crash test energy while keeping the passenger cell intact, but this was simply not available. In the end they had to make do with

11.8–13.8in/300–350mm, and somehow managed to reach every required standard.

That apparently focussed the attention of the engineers, who somehow found extra free crush space elsewhere – there is very clever packaging of the engine around the bulkhead, which is recessed to suit, and they even found some crush space behind the line of the front wheels. Clever.

The new car's style was settled before the end of 1996, a great credit to the team at Rover who refined the original Frank Stephenson theme, and steered it through and around all the conflicting artistic and technical obstacles. Those of you who have already sampled the car sometimes whinge about the lack of interior space, but both BMW and Rover Group (who did the job from 1996 to 1999) stoutly defend the combination of (they say) 'drop-dead gorgeous' looks, practicality and the low-roof theme.

Continuity – continuity with the old,

One of the features of the Mini style was a roof line which appears to rise slightly towards the tail. This was an illusion, but nevertheless it emphasises just how shallow the rear quarter windows actually are. The impression of enormous wheels (these, in fact, are 16in alloys) was quite definitely intended. Look, too, at the profile of the bonnet as it flows over the cooling radiator in the nose – it is not nearly as sloping as one originally might think.

From every angle, both Rover and BMW tried to make the new MINI give the impression of being an evolution of the old. Designers asked themselves: 'What would the old Mini have looked like by 2000 if there had been a new generation every ten years or so?'

that is – also had to be preserved. Gert Hildebrand, who led the MINI design team from 2000 – makes that point very strongly: 'We had to make the new car hark back to the old one. If you are going to spend more than DM30,000 (£10,000) on a car, there must be constancy. The downfall of other car companies is that there is sometimes no constancy in their products. When you want to build up a brand, when you change a model, you can't go far away from a certain feeling, a certain impression which people already have of the car. It would make no sense to make a MINI that looks completely different from what people had in mind about the old Mini. On the new MINI, you recognise from the old, the 1959 car, the same round headlamps, the same front grille, which smiles at you, the same steep windscreen. Even the same line of the welded seam which lines up with the windscreen – on the new car there is a panel gap.'

For all those reasons, several Classic Mini styling cues have been retained. The

boxy, four-square proportions, the wheel-at-each-corner stance, the flat roof line and the near straight waistline are all familiar. Even the windscreen angle was treated as an 'icon' – new and old are virtually the same – while the so-familiar exposed front panel seams of the original Mini, which pointed down from the screen to the front-wheels, have been retained as panel gaps on the new car. That particular line appeared on just about every concept – Spiritual or E50 MINI – which was developed in the 1994–1995 period. Sometimes as a pressings joint, sometimes a feature and sometimes only a pastiche – it seemed to be a 'given', and survived to be featured on the production cars.

The 'clam-shell' bonnet pressing, complete with its 'I'm so cute' headlamps, was another feature which every designer seemed to accept. Gert Hildebrand suggested that this is how the 'missing generations' of Classic Mini would naturally have evolved. The Rover design team agreed with this, and there was never

any doubt that they would be adopted.

But, 'clam-shell' or not, should the entire front end be a lift-up assembly, or should there be a big centre panel and fixed wings? That was a ticklish problem, and one which was only finally settled when the question of engine bay access was considered – and when the feasibility of pressing such a massive panel was settled.

The end result was a striking style, a three-door car with a quite startlingly stiff structure. Dr Heinrich Petra made the point that a car intended to handle extremely well would need an ultra-solid structure, and that BMW was always determined to provide one: 'The MINI has one of the stiffest body structures BMW has ever designed – at about 24,500Nm/degree its torsional strength is equal to that of the latest 3-Series. It is much stiffer than the old Classic Mini, much stiffer than had ever before been achieved at Rover.'

In fact, 27,000Nm/degree was the initial target, but not even BMW engineers are superhuman, and the production-achieved figure still towers above the 9,000Nm/degree achieved with the Rover 200 hatchback.

The oily bits ...

BMW's concept engineers had already decided that the new car should be conventional, by current front-wheel-drive standards. The engine would be transversely mounted, the five-speed gearbox would be mounted alongside it and to its left, front suspension would be by coil springs and MacPherson struts, there would be power-assisted rack-and-pinion steering, and independent rear suspension would be a more compact form of BMW's complex, but celebrated, 'Z-axle'.

Does this mean that Rover Group found itself with little to do except refine those concepts? Not at all, for very little detail engineering work had been done. No ready-developed parts, incidentally, were likely to be available from a 'parts bin' – neither at Longbridge nor in Munich.

Until I saw the MINI in the flesh, I wasn't sure about the style, but one day's driving was enough to convince me. It looks sporty, cheeky even, from every angle.
(David Wigmore)

61

The MINI's front-end body structure was engineered to expose the entire engine bay when the huge one-piece bonnet was raised. The front bumper moulding was almost the last component to be added at the assembly stage, with the radiators tucked close up behind it. The light-coloured aluminium casting is one of the engine mountings, and the five-speed transmission is tucked away, out of sight, under the air cleaner box.
(David Wigmore)

Some of the MINI's styling details are exquisitely conceived. There are no fewer than three separate lamp lenses behind the single glass cover, with extra low-level lights positioned in the main swelling of the bumper moulding.
(David Wigmore)

'One of the first things we did,' Griffin told me, 'was to change the gearbox, which didn't go down very well! BMW had wanted the car to have a Getrag gearbox, but we put in the R65 gearbox instead, because it was £100/car cheaper, more compact with a two-shaft as opposed to a three-shaft layout, and no inherent cyclic vibrations, so a mass damper was not needed.'

Because the design of the front-wheel-drive Rover 75 had already been finalised around a new-generation Getrag gearbox – BMW had been patronising this German specialist for more than three decades – the proposed link-up was logical, but the British didn't see it that way. The Getrag box, which would be all-new, would necessarily be costly and take time to develop.

The R65, on the other hand, was an existing major component, which was already being manufactured on the Longbridge site, and was in large scale use in other Rover Group front-wheel-drive cars. Originally a PSA (Peugeot-Citroën) design, it was well-proven, and well thought of.

Unhappily, it took Rover Group ages to convince BMW that this should be done, as there seemed to be a growing culture in Germany which (to alter George Orwell) stated: 'German engineering Good, British engineering Bad.' To many over-worked British engineers, it seemed, they saw an attitude which suggested that the only acceptable method was the BMW method.

On this occasion, though, Chris Lee's team stuck to its convictions, produced rafts of evidence regarding costs, performance and service experience. Back-to-back tests, evaluations on the road and comparisons of torque capacities were all made. In addition, major improvements to the R65's change quality, a reduction of free play and healthy attention to warranty claim records were all needed before Rover won the argument.

Then, when the Cooper S derivative came along, the R65 couldn't cope with its increased torque, and BMW had to choose a 6-speed Getrag gearbox after all ...'

On the other hand, although Dr Alex Moulton continually pressed Rover Group to adopt his latest, cheaper and more compact Hydragas suspension systems, the team never seriously considered choosing it in place of coil springs and conventional dampers: 'Hydragas needs to have ways of being replenished at garages,' Griffin reminded me, 'which isn't customer-friendly these days, or cheap, either for the customer or the garage. We were content to go with steel springs instead, and they do a reasonable job ...'

There was an attempt, even then, to install a Honda-inspired coil spring/double wishbone layout, with which Rover was already familiar on the 200 (later 25), but that was soon abandoned.

At the rear, the operation of the Z-axle, which had already been adopted for the still-secret Rover 75 project, was never in any doubt (the author has lived with such systems in BMWs for some years ...) but initially it was too bulky, and compromised the amount of space in the rear cabin. Much detail work was needed – by Rover Group, not by BMW – to make it more compact, and to make it 'package' better; the outcome being a much shallower installation than on any other BMWs.

Design, as much as Engineering, suffered agonies over this, for until the Z-axle was put on a diet, it encroached significantly on the available boot (trunk) space, and on the rear seat construction. The finalised layout, as used on the hundreds of MINIs now being built every day at Oxford, minimised such intrusions.

By the summer of 1996, therefore, the basic engineering layout of the new R50 had been agreed, and thought was already being given to getting a prototype on to the road. Yet there were two major areas yet to be covered. The interior, in particular the fascia and instrument layout, was one.

The other, vital to everything else connected with the car, was the engine. Quite simply, there wasn't one!

BMW saw certain styling 'cues' from the Classic Mini as important. This explains why the bonnet/body shut line is at exactly the same angle as the MINI's windscreen pillar, just as it was in 1959. (David Wigmore)

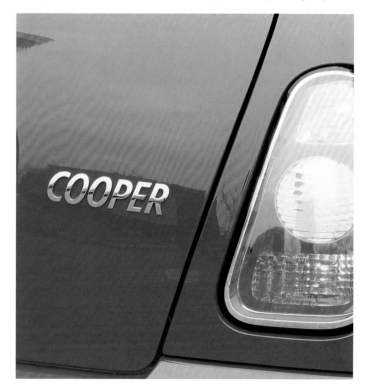

'Cooper' became a famous name in connection with the original Mini, and BMW made sure it would be present in the new MINI range. Look at the hatchback, but not the bonnet, to get the good news ... (David Wigmore)

4 Previews
and publicity
Setting the scene

So, what could be done about the engine? Even after the body style and the basic chassis engineering had been settled by the late summer of 1996, no engine – not even the envelope (outline) of an engine – had been chosen for the car. Although it is simplistic to suggest that all original layout sketches merely drew a box with the word 'engine' inside it, there was little else to go on. In fact there was no positive news of any type until September 1996, when BMW Powertrain told the project team in the UK what to expect.

In the beginning, BMW considered producing a new engine coded M14, but that existed only on paper, was meant for in-line, front-engine/rear-drive usage, and would have been very difficult to package. Although the Z13 project car had used a four-cylinder water-cooled BMW motorcycle engine, this was not thought suitable either.

So, if the new MINI was slated to be assembled at Longbridge, why not slot the celebrated Rover K-Series power units into the engine bay? The engines, after all, were manufactured on site, in considerable numbers, and little capital investment would have been needed to adapt them for the MINI.

The K-Series, after all, had already been used in cars as diverse as the Rover 100 and the MGF, they were being made in sizes spanning 1.1 and 1.8-litres, with 8-valve or 16-valve heads, and with power outputs from 75bhp to 160bhp. So, what was the problem?

Here now, is an abiding mystery. The K-Series, it seems, was rejected because it was too large – too bulky, too high, too long, choose your own definition – which clashes directly with the fact that Rover Group's engineers had been able to fit one into the Minki project car of 1994, while only widening the original Classic Mini structure by two inches.

Not that this swayed any one of several opinions which I received from the principal characters. Dr Petra said that along with the British R65 gearbox, it was physically too big, too wide, while Chris Lee said that the engine/transmission *could* have been inserted, but 'not without us making significant changes to the concept. It was too wide – too wide, that is, across the engine bay of the motorcar.'

So be it. Although Rover Group had re-engineered the Metro in 1990 to take the K-Series engine, and Minki tells its own story, the same transplant was never even considered for the R50. To this day, though, I think there may be some sort of hidden agenda …

Although this was the period when BMW was also preparing to build a new range of NG42 (New Generation 4-Cylinder) engines at a factory at Hams Hall in the UK, these were to be 1.8-litre and 2.0-litre types, were currently intended for use in larger BMWs, and Rover cars like the 25, 45 and the Land Rover Freelander.

Larger and more sophisticated than needed for the MINI, and quite incapable of

Once the first representative prototypes were completed, in 1997/1998, testing took place in Europe's coldest territories – mainly in Sweden and Finland. With lots of snow on the ground, it was important to assess the low-grip handling.

The MINI Cooper's fascia/instrument display is ultra-modern but, as the designers insist, the use of a central speedometer and open parcel shelves is a nod to tradition too.

This moody picture shows the way that the MINI Cooper's instrument display is lit up, at night.

being fitted into the R50's engine bay, they were not even considered for use in the new model. Eventually it was Wolfgang Reitzle who dialled up his world-wide connections, homed in on François Castaing at Chrysler in Detroit, and suggested that a new joint-project engine design might work well for both parties.

Informal talks lead to formal negotiations, and it seems that the timing could not have been more nicely-timed. Chrysler (who were still independent of Daimler-Benz at that stage), were looking to launch a series of new front-wheel-drive models, such as the revised Neon and the PT Cruiser. It already had an existing 2.0-litre power unit, but was interested in adding a smaller, less powerful, engine to those ranges.

The result was that Chrysler agreed to design a brand-new engine, coded W10, which would be for their own use, and that of BMW. Like Chrysler's existing, larger, 2.0-litre power unit, it would be a 16-valver, though this time there would only be a single overhead camshaft. Initially Chrysler stated that it was meant to be produced in 1.4-litre and 1.6-litre sizes (though by 2002 no 'entry-level' 1.4-litre engine had yet been seen in public, certainly not on a MINI). In public, at least, this W10 design became the new 'Pentagon' power unit. As always intended, it was already in full production and use by both corporations before the end of 2001.

But, where to build it? In Germany, in the UK, or in Austria (many BMW engines are produced at Steyr, in Austria)? After extensive economic analysis had been done, it was decided to set up a new joint venture (BMW and Chrysler would share the investment in a company called Tritec Motors Ltda) in a manufacturing plant at Camp Largo, in Brazil, where labour costs would be low (much lower than for a similar plant set up in Great Britain or Germany) and planning permission was easy to secure. Eberhard Schrempf would be the plant's first Managing Director.

Nothing in the MINI instrument/controls package is conventional, or looks old-fashioned – this being the chunky little column stalks, complete with rotating drum controls.

The centre console on the MINI Cooper housed the ventilation system (air conditioning was optional), the radio/CD installation and a row of switches which controlled electric window lifts and auxiliary lights.

Clever factory photography makes it look as if there is ample rear seat space for two passengers. In truth, with normal-sized passengers in the front seats, there is very little leg room indeed behind them.

Until the 1970s, Brazil's motor industry was distinctly backward. It was only after multi-national companies like Ford, GM, Fiat and VW moved in, attracted by the ample supply of labour, the low cost of building land, and the wide choice of venues, that things began to change. By the year 2000, Brazil was not only producing major components for other companies, but it was also building nearly 1.4 million cars every year, many of them being lightly modified, up-to-date, versions of models such as the VW Golf and the Ford Fiesta. BMW, therefore, was not taking a big gamble by locating its new engine factory in Brazil, but merely joining a well-established trend.

Engines, it was decided, would be supplied to the UK in containers by the shipload. This 300-acre factory was to be ready to run early in 2000, when MINI

assembly was expected to begin. When MINI production had been fully expanded, BMW agreed to take up to 200,000 units in a full year, while Chrysler hoped to match that with their own requirements. In the first phase, only 300 workers would be needed to build 250,000 engines a year for the two clients, and 400,000 units a year, in the future, was certainly a feasible target.

Before the engine could be designed, though, Rover Group's engineers thought that Chrysler needed to know more about Minis. What sort of a car was the Mini? What sort of a car should a new Mini be? What about the characters, and how should an engine be related to that?

'In Detroit, where excitement was needed,' Chris Lee explained, 'they were more used to working on big and powerful V8 and V10 engines. Neons and PT Cruisers; well, they were utility products.

68

We spent a lot of time explaining what the spirit of the new MINI would be all about, that although this car would be small, it should also be exciting to drive. We even gave them a couple of Classic Minis – we exported a couple to them in Auburn Hills – for them to get the flavour of Mini motoring. The Mini, you see, hadn't been sold in the USA for 30 years, so it was only fanatics who knew anything about them.'

For the next 18 months there was regular contact with Chrysler – not only BMW Powertrain of Munich, but the Rover Group engineering team – which involved regular flights to and from Detroit, regular meetings, and a gradual recognition that Chrysler could do a great job: 'On paper the specification looked pretty ordinary – it had a cast iron block, and a single overhead camshaft – and originally we were concerned about that.

We then found that the Chrysler guys were a real bunch of enthusiasts. Many of them had already worked on the Viper sports cars, so we soon realised that they were real petrolheads. Very professional, very quick to understand what was wanted, very fast in what they did, and always having a great deal of fun ...'

Both Rover Group and Chrysler agreed that they wanted to see one of the most cost-effective, zestful and physical small 1.6-litre engines in the world – one that should cost only 'nickels and dimes'. Right from the start, downsizing and packaging everything was critically important, as Chris Lee recalls: 'Americans are usually not short of useful free crush space on their cars, but we were. We had to say: "If you continue to configure this engine with its various ancillaries – air-conditioning compressors, alternators, power steering

Access to the rear seats on the MINI, which is, after all, a three-door hatchback, was not easy. Once installed – and if there was leg space – the seats were surprisingly comfortable.

69

The MINI's new engine was designed by Chrysler in Detroit. Called the 'Pentagon' unit, it was a 16-valver with single-overhead camshaft.

In order to keep as much free 'crush space' as possible in the engine bay, the engineers arranged for all the engine ancillaries (pumps, alternators and starter motor) to be on the same side of the transversely-located power unit.

pumps, fuel injection equipment – on the front face and on the back face, in other words on both sides of the engine, then you are using up all our under-bonnet air space, which will tend to "strut out" and go solid too early in the crash pulse.

'They said: "But it will cost an awful lot of money to move all the ancillaries on to one face …" – so we had to say: "Not as much as it will cost us to re-engineer the structure of the car!" In the end we had to get very firm about this problem, and were successful. It was mission-critical to the MINI – and it worked.

'In the end, we saw the first genuinely driveable prototype engines in the summer/autumn of 1997 – we had some very early engines sent across from Detroit – and we were pleasantly surprised by the way they drove, and by what they sounded like. Even though the specification still sounded ho-hum, and the engines were not producing the required power, the experience looked promising.'

In the end, the only major feature on which the companies agreed to disagree was that BMW wanted to use variable valve timing technology (and advertise its presence) while Chrysler's engineers did not. Major arguments, discussion papers and presentations solved nothing, and in the end it was a BMW steering committee which backed down, and the proposal was abandoned.

On the road

Fully-engineered prototype cars would not – could not – be ready before the end of 1997, but in the meantime Rover Group needed to gain experience of their new model. Well before Programme Approval was due – in January 1998 – more road work was needed, and this was where the well-known industry practice of building 'mules' came into play.

Happily for the British, a new-generation Rover 200 hatchback had been launched at the end of 1995, so chassis work could begin even before body shells, and especially engines, were available.

Accordingly, the very first 'mules' to be created were actually much-modified Rover 200s, reduced in weight to the target weight of MINI, with re-tuned K-Series engines to give representative power – and with much stiffened structures.

Because the R50 was meant to be impressively stiff, and the Rover 200, though creditable enough, was good for only 9,000Nm/degree in torsion, it was necessary to rig out these cars with full rally-type roll cages to stop the shells racking around more than desired.

Real prototypes – those cars which not only combined the new platform with the intended style, and first examples of the 'Pentagon' engine – did not actually take to the road until late 1997, which explains why ever-active industry 'spies' never got a sighting of the style until it appeared – very briefly – on the eve of the Frankfurt Motor Show in September 1997.

This totally-premature pre-launch explains why so many Mini-watchers (including the author) thought that the programme was being dragged out. It was not – in fact it was going ahead remarkably swiftly – but the preliminaries had already been talked up at great length, by those inside and outside the Rover Group.

As early as May 1997, even before proper prototypes had gone on to the road, BMW had started a controlled leaking process. Although they deny it now, at the time, and later in the year, BMW carried out a classic spoiling exercise, which was successfully meant to take attention away from the imminent arrival of the new Mercedes-Benz A-Class.

The 'smoke and mirrors' appearance of totally irrelevant cars like ACV30 (January 1997) and Spiritual (March 1997) had whetted people's appetites, as had the remarks of BMW's recently-installed chief

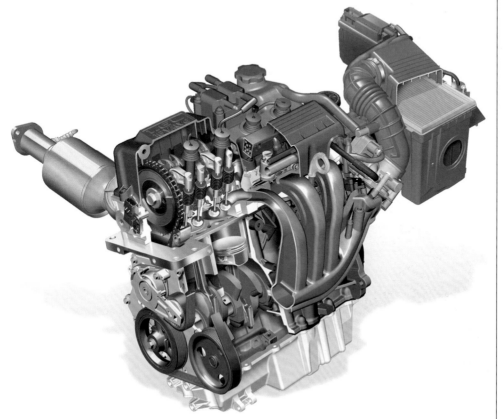

A cutaway drawing of the original version of the all-new 'Pentagon' engine for the MINI, later to be shared with Chrysler Neon and PT Cruiser models. The new Brazilian-built 1.6-litre engine was very compact, very light, with a 16-valve layout.

Like the original Mini of 1959, the BMW-backed MINI of 2001 had a transverse-engine and front-wheel-drive layout, but was much larger and totally different in detail. New features included a hatchback style and the much-praised BMW 'Z-axle' type of independent rear suspension.

executive at Rover, Dr Walter Hasselkus. Admitting that a new MINI was being developed, he commented that: 'We and Mercedes-Benz will be the first to sell small cars at premium prices. It certainly won't be where the current Mini now sits. It will be bigger, for safety. We don't want a minimum car any more, for profit and image reasons …'

Later in the year, Dr Hasselkus also made a remark which would come to haunt him: 'The new MINI could only be a Rover …' – a promise which rapidly unravelled when BMW divested itself of the Rover Group in 2000.

Official news of the new car's style came in September 1997, when two exterior photographs – a three-quarter-front and a three-quarter-rear – of a red-and-white MINI-Cooper were circulated. Although Rover Group and BMW admitted to a planned launch in late 2000 (which was to

be *three* years after this preview, an unprecedented gap), the technical information provided was sparse. There were no under-bonnet views, and none of the interior. At the time, we thought that this was for reasons of security – but now (as I have already explained) we know that this is because neither item was fitted to a viewable car!

Front-wheel-drive with a transversely-mounted engine was a 'given', and it was agreed that the engine would be an all-new 1.6-litre 16-valver from Chrysler, and there would be more than one tune. As in the past, 'basic' (this would later be finalised as 'One') and more powerful Cooper versions would go on sale. At this time, and not until 2000, no exterior dimensions (neither wheelbase nor length) were quoted, nor was the wheel size, and nor were any horsepower figures.

One week later, Rover Group and BMW

stunned the media for arranging for a Mini prototype to drive into – and immediately out of – what had been offered as a static presentation of what was to follow in 2000. It was the same car as that for which pictures had just been published and, as before, no technical details were released. And it was almost, but not quite, a hoax because: 'Very little of that car was real,' Brian Griffin now admits. 'It was only what we called an "experience car", or a "skin prototype". These are done in our industry by picking a car that is nearest in size to what is being designed, and converting it visibly – exterior and interior – to represent the actual car. That was done in late 1996/early 1997 – they were very early running test cars – and they were based on the modified platform and running gear of a Fiat Punto, with a Punto engine and gearbox!'

One group of motoring writers, at least, got close to the truth. Top design chief Geoff Upex was asked what engine was in the car they had just seen, and when he replied that of course it was all Top Secret, and that of course he could make no comment, the response was: 'Funny, that, it

sounded just like a Fiat ...'

Not that this sort of controversy troubled BMW one bit, for they had successfully previewed their intentions for the new car, and at the same time they had diverted the publicity which would otherwise have gone to the new Mercedes-Benz A-Class and MCC Smart cars.

Behind the scenes, too, not only had all the initial engineering work been completed, but the style of the interior had been settled. Although this aspect of the car had barely been started when the project was handed over to Rover Group in 1996, Dave Saddington's interior design team, led by Wyn Thomas and Tony Hunter, picked up the problem, assessed what was needed, rapidly developed the agreed layout and had it approved by British and German management. The very first 'experience car' to be completed with a total, as-proposed, interior, was based on a Rover 200 platform.

Although there seemed to be superficial similarities with ACV30's fascia, the two developed independently of each other: 'If you were doing an evolutionary Mini, what else would you do but look at the top

Both front and rear suspension assemblies in the new Mini were carried on stout sub-frames. At the front there was a conventional MacPherson strut layout, the power-assisted steering rack also being carried on the crossmember. At the rear, Rover's engineers managed to minimise the height and sheer bulk of BMW's celebrated Z-axle rear suspension.

Multi-
national
links

When BMW revealed that the new MINI would use a newly-developed DaimlerChrysler engine, which would be manufactured in a joint-venture business in Brazil, few people even raised an eyebrow at the news. By this time there were so many cross-border, cross-company deals in place in the world's motor industry that this latest one was not considered to break any new ground.

Yet as far as BMW was concerned, this was indeed a novelty. Every previous BMW engine had been an in-house BMW design, manufactured either in Germany or in a 100 per cent BMW-owned factory in Austria or Great Britain.

As far as BMW was concerned, this merely added to the massive spider's web of modern worldwide trade and manufacturing arrangements for which the motor industry is now famous.

BMWs were already being built in the USA for sale around the world, while BMWs built in South Africa also found a multitude of homes.

Following the separation of the companies, many other parts for the new MINI were being supplied by so-called 'competitors', including major body pressings from Land Rover (which has been Ford-owned since 2000). In addition, the R65-type five-speed transmission was built on the MG Rover site at Longbridge (though BMW had retained the rights to that design).

BMW's 'Z-axle' independent rear suspension system was first seen on late-1980s BMWs, and has since been applied to many other models. For the MINI, although the principle was the same as before – and there were as many links, bushes, springs and dampers – its size, and particularly its height, were cleverly minimised.

The registration plate of this black prototype, still with incorrect headlamp detailing, tells us that it was a very early British-built MINI, probably being tested on ice and snow for the very first time, in 1998. No badges, and some disguise, of course.

"crash" roll, look at something like a centre speedometer and look at something like an open shelf ...'

And, indeed, there was an open shelf under the fascia itself, and I am assured that the wide panel gaps between dashboard pressing and instruments were meant to be like that. But was there any justification for mounting the rev counter of the Cooper behind the steering wheel, where the top sweep of the needle simply cannot be seen by a relatively tall driver?

There were, indeed, oddities at all angles. Door glass was frameless, which is usually a recipe for wind noise and leaks – yet clever detailing (as I found on test cars) ensured that this did not occur. The fascia style might have been plain, but the door

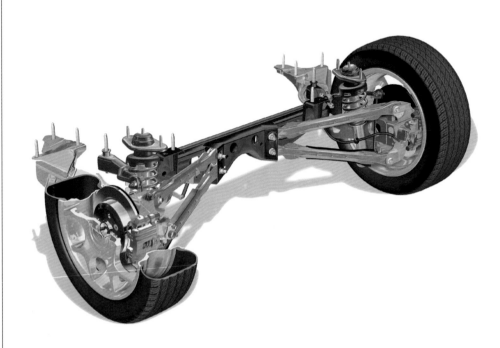

M̲ini̲ testing in cold conditions in Scandinavia. These were fully engineered prototypes, with the finalised body style and fittings. The bicycle wheel is actually an accurate speed measuring device.

furniture was a real mixture – plain, plain trim panels, but a three-piece light-alloy door pull which effectively blocked off access to the depth of the pockets. Electric window lifts – on a M̲ini̲? Air conditioning as an option – on a M̲ini̲? An adjustable steering column – on a M̲ini̲? This, for sure, was not like the old Mini, but much more like my idea of a new, small BMW. But it was not, repeat not, badged as a BMW, and the parent company would

never let me forget that …

Even so, this was a thoroughly modern, forward-looking fascia and interior. Older motoring writers later found it difficult to come to terms with a display which was totally at odds, not only with what BMW was doing with its own-brand cars, but with what they had approved for use in the Rover 75 of the same artistic period.

In marketing speak, however, it was

apparently funky, youthful, fun, forward-looking and life-style-orientated – all of which were attributes that BMW would later add to its marketing platform.

In the meantime, preparation work for putting the car into production was already forging ahead. Having spent ages trying to decide whether to modernise Longbridge … or to modernise Cowley … or to close Longbridge … or none of these, BMW elected to pump squillions into the

Longbridge site. The official figure for MINI investment was £400 million – but by the time BMW pulled the plug in March 2000, that figure had surely been passed.

West Works at Longbridge, where body-in-white (this is an industry expression for unpainted, unprotected, body shells in their raw, as-welded-together state) assembly would take place, from panels supplied by specialists including the one-time Pressed Steel Fisher plant in Swindon, would be re-

For cold-weather testing of the definitive cars, BMW established its own permanent test buildings. With outside temperatures sometimes as low as −40°C, the availability of warm workshops was welcome!

Full instrumentation and data logging is the norm with today's prototypes. This MINI prototype was being tested in Scandinavian winter conditions, but the same sort of data logging would also be needed in ultra-hot weather tests.

jigged, initially by ditching the ageing Rover 100 facility, and by installing new robotised lines in its place. As with existing models, bodies would be supplied from West Works to the main Longbridge ('East Works') complex by overhead conveyor, and plans were also laid to reserve a modern assembly hall for the MINI.

At a meeting with the labour unions in July 1997, Bernd Pischetsrieder promised that the new MINI would go into production late in 1999. This was a white lie for, among themselves, BMW already knew that it could not be ready until a year later. This was enough, however, to get the workforce 'on side', and keep them sweet while restructuring went ahead.

This was vital. With Classic Mini sales stumbling peacefully towards the end of the century – only 20,051 had been sold in 1995, and all the trends pointed

downwards – BMW was much more ambitious for the new-generation car.

By 1998, when a third derivative, the Cooper S, had been added to the proposed range of hatchbacks (but there was still no definite thought of adding other body derivatives), the parent company was forecasting that 127,000 MINIs would be built in the first full calendar year, building up to a peak of 172,000 in the second year, then falling away very gradually to 131,000 in 2005 and 86,000 in 2007. If these figures were to be attained, Longbridge would once again be full – for the first time since the strike-ridden 1970s.

Even at that stage, the original E50/MINI was forecast to have an eight year life – this was also a normal turnover rate for other BMW models – in which close to a million cars would be produced. The forecast was that 450,000 of these would be 'One' types,

411,000 would be 'Cooper' and 118,000 would be 'Cooper S'. In total, of this million, BMW thought that 185,000 would be sold in the UK, 236,000 in Germany, 104,000 in Italy, 195,000 in the rest of Europe and 87,000 in Japan.

Significantly, the decision to market the cars in the United States had already been taken, where forecast sales in eight years were 109,000, of which 82,500 would be Coopers. Even so, in 1999 there were proposals to eliminate the USA from the sales proposals, this only being reinstated a year later. Gradually, though not drastically, BMW was obliged to downgrade these projections, especially when the challenge of developing a new brand – this was not just to be a new Rover model, but a new stand-alone brand – were quantified. And it was not only inside the business that the changes had to come, but also out in the wide world.

During the Scandinavian winter, frozen lakes can prove surprisingly useful when cold testing MINI prototypes.

John Cooper, the legendary character who lent his name to the original Mini-Cooper in 1961, was introduced to the new MINI Cooper in August 1998. Pictured here in the secure viewing garden in the Gaydon Design Centre, John saw just how much larger the new car was, compared with the old one which his name helped to make so famous.

There would be different, but parallel routes. In the UK, BMW decided, MINIs would be sold by existing Rover (not BMW) dealers, who would be urged (coerced, more likely) to develop separate showrooms and service organisations. In the rest of the world, MINIs would be handled by BMW franchises.

Gradually, but so subtly that many pundits did not realise that they were being used to pre-condition the clientele, BMW let slip a few details about the cars. They would be built at Longbridge. They would be separately branded. They would not only be larger but rather more costly than the Classic Mini. They would aim to be 'lifestyle' cars, not runabouts. They would carry a youthful, trendy image. They were intended to be fun to drive, and fun to own. They were intended to have industry-leading handling. In particular, they were expected to have 'go kart' characteristics.

Accidentally-on-purpose, or so it seemed, disguised prototypes just happened to be caught when out testing. The existence of a Cooper version had already been confirmed at Frankfurt in September 1997, but by 1998 the first rumours, never

denied, of a proposed Cooper S derivative also began to circulate, and Rover 200-bodied 'mules' were seen, out on test. Here was a derivative, the stories trumpeted, which would have a supercharged (not turbocharged) engine which would produce at least 150bhp, and give the new car a 135mph top speed.

Except that the forecasts of a simultaneous launch with other MINIs were proved to be wrong, this was more or less what a Cooper S was meant to do. But how did it come about?

'On one of his regular visits to Gaydon,' Chris Lee told me, 'Wolfgang Reitzle visited the design studio with me, looked out into the viewing garden, and asked: "Why is that 200 out there?"

"It's for you to drive."

"I don't want to drive it."

"You will. It's a 'mule'. Would you like to drive it and tell us what it is?"

'He drove straight out on to the test track, was out for 30 minutes – so long that we thought, oh Gawd he must have crashed it – then he came back with a huge smile on his face. You don't get that often from him. He walked back to me, and he said,

"Heiss," – which is German for 'spicy' or 'hot' – "that's the Cooper S!" Paper presentations don't always work, but show them a one-off prototype and you can win their hearts and minds with that. Which is what we did with the Cooper S …'

Testing, testing …

By 1997 and 1998 the R50 programme had built up a colossal momentum all of its own, and Rover had already taken the trouble to introduce the new car to the man who gave his name to one version – John Cooper. This legendary figure in the British motoring establishment, who had not only built World Championship-winning F1 cars in the 1950s and 1960s, but had inspired the birth of the very first Mini-Cooper in 1961, was also a long-established motor trader (close to Worthing, in Sussex) with a Mini franchise, and a thriving tuning operation.

Having been introduced to the new car – and being the subject of poignant pictures, where he posed between old-type and new-type models – John was delighted to see that all the character, the response and the fun-potential of the original had somehow

been bred in to the new car. Even BMW's own staff, who naturally knew less about this great man than did the Rover Group team, was pleased with his response.

Although John was also privileged to see the car introduced to its public in 2000, unhappily he died just before the end of the year, when the car had not yet gone on sale. But his name lives on …

By the autumn of 1996, about 120 people had been gathered together to work on the R50 project (that included everyone from the programme director down to the tea boy and the office cat), while all the concept work had been agreed, frozen and sent forward for detailing in the winter of 1996/1997, and the first 'Pentagon' engines arrived during 1997.

As more and more detail was settled, and had to be 'drawn up' (or should I say 'created' on a 3D-configured computer?), the numbers continued to rise. In 1998, more and more BMW specialists were drafted in from Munich, so that by 1999, when BMW abruptly decided to take the near-complete project back to Germany once again, at least 500 Rover staff were

To their credit, BMW was always determined to add the famous 'Cooper' name to the line up of models in the new Mini range. Here, in August 1998, John Cooper himself met one of the first Mini Cooper prototypes to be completed, and was flattered to be consulted thereafter at every stage of the development of the new car. Note the snap-action fuel filler cap – which would not be adopted on production cars. Rover design was always unhappy about that deletion.

Work on the new Chrysler-designed 'Pentagon' engine did not begin until 1996, well after the new MINI's exterior style had been settled. Limiting the engine width was critical, for there was not excessive space between the body panels surrounding the MacPherson strut towers. Rover's very successful K-Series engine, we were assured, simply would not fit into this space.

totally involved in the project. Chris Lee was obliged to hand over control of the project, briefly to Peter Morgan (who had been involved with the Rover 75), but from June 1999 it came under the control of Dr Heinrich Petra once again. BMW-Munich was now in total control.

As had Lee in 1996, Dr Petra now had to set up a new office and staff in Munich, which totalled 70 members by the time the car was in production: 'We offered all the project members in Gaydon the chance to join us [in Munich]. Of course, that would have meant them having to learn German.' And in the end just two Brits moved to Germany to continue their links with this car.

Although the peak of MINI creative work was over by the end of 1997, the sheer hard graft of engineering, testing, development and releasing had then to be tackled.

Everyone remembers this as a tough assignment, not only technically, but in timing terms – for there were never any doubts that it would *have* to be ready on time. Except for its R65 gearbox, incidentally, Rover Group engineers reminded me that it really was an *all* new car (new engine, new structure, new style, new suspension and new technological systems), which is really a rarity in the British motor industry.

At this stage there was the added problem of having to come to terms with the BMW way of assembling cars, rather than what can be called the 'Honda method', which had gradually become standard at Longbridge during the 1990s. The difference was mainly in the way – the sequence and the progressing – that body pressings and structures were put together, but as the same new standards were being applied to the Rover 75 (which was just

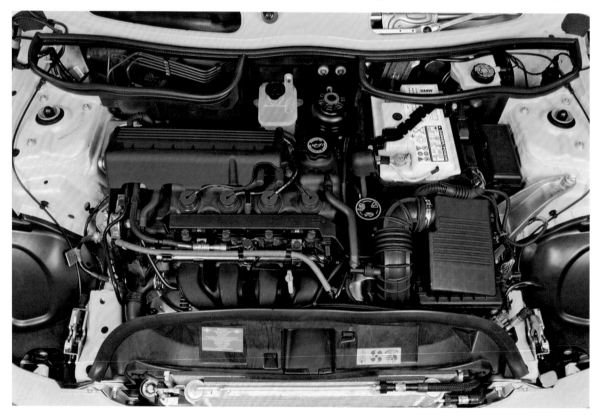

about to go into volume production at Cowley), many Rover Group people were familiar with this.

Slowly, painfully even, at first, the number of real prototypes began to increase, and were put to use. The numbers, which had seemed to be manageable in the 1980s, had now rocketed – not out of control, but certainly into the stratosphere. The days when a mere 20 cars would suffice were long gone. Even though they were operating on a very tight financial basis, this was a period

when the Rover Group had upwards of 1,000 prototype, test and experimental cars on its books.

For the MINI project alone, by the autumn of 1998 there were already up to 100 cars on strength – 42 cars that either looked like new MINIS or were heavily disguised MINIS, along with many 'experience cars' and 'mules'. At least 20 of them would eventually have to be subjected to crash tests of one type or another. In the second phase, when many 'off-tools' components would be available, the project

Though cars can be designed on a computer, they must be developed on the road. No amount of high-tech electronics can take the place of driving expertise. How, for example, would the MINI handle on tightening tarmac corners?
(David Wigmore)

83

team was planning to produce a further 99 cars and five body shells, of which a total of 18 would be subjected to one or other of the severe barrier crash tests.

'These were expensive beasts,' Brian Griffin states. 'So they tended to be multi-tasked wherever possible. Even so, BMW always told us that they could have done the job with fewer cars than we were using – yet their engineering budget covered a grand total of 3,500 vehicles!'

However, there were still problems – major problems which could only be resolved by the spending of much time, money and team effort. Even though high-speed runs on the old Nürburgring race circuit were completed successfully – 5,000 miles/8000 km at an average lap time of 9min 40sec on the legendary old 'Nordschleife', the car was still not right. Specifically, prototypes were all coming out overweight, under-powered and looking to cost too much. This became obvious when the R50 was subjected to its first major management 'ride-and-drive' exercise, in Sardinia in October 1998.

Having launched the new-generation (E46) 3-Series saloons in carefully controlled surroundings (wonderful weather, a varied and demanding test route and reasonably secure from media interference), BMW elected to hold a VIF (Vorstand Informations Fahrt) on the same site.

This, effectively, was where BMW and Rover Group top management gathered to assess a number of products that were either reaching production, or those that were at significant phases in their product development. It was an ideal time, therefore, for the very latest R50/MINI prototypes to be tried out.

'We were still running with some incomplete details in terms of the cabin,' Chris Lee told me. 'They were very happy with the car, up to that point in its development, but everyone was disappointed with the shortcomings of the "Pentagon" engines. We were still not seeing engines with the driveability we wanted – it wasn't a question of a performance shortfall.

Even the standard MINI Cooper's engine bay (this car) looks well packed, but add the supercharger of a Cooper S, its intercooler, plus air-conditioning, and suddenly there is no space left. (David Wigmore)

'The biggest question was that our prototypes were coming out much heavier than the target weights, and that was having a major effect on the handling. It was of grave concern to the Board members, and it starkly exposed that problem – I remember that most clearly.'

At this point the Board members must have been appalled. On this test, the 'entry-level' One (which was loaded up with specification extras such as air conditioning, satellite navigation and test gear) weighed in at 1,165kg instead of the 995kg target, while the 1.6-litre engine was delivering 83bhp instead of the target of 90bhp. In crude terms, this made the power/weight ratio no less than 22 per cent below par.

If ever there was a mid-term crisis in the MINI project, this was it. At a time when BMW was launching the Rover 75 to the world at the Birmingham Motor Show, and when top management was telling the world of the problems which still faced the Rover Group, this dramatic (but unpublicised) failure of the new MINI to

Rev-counter detail on the MINI Cooper. The outside temperature gauge, safety belt wearer's warning and other lights are all there, before the driver's eyes.
(David Wigmore)

impress its sponsors was not welcome.

Rover Group and (if they ever admitted it) their opposite numbers in Munich knew that such problems always strike a new car at one time or another, and were confident that all could be overcome – but would they be given time?

To quote the title of a pop song current at the time: 'Things Can Only Get Better'. But could they?

Do you remember how uncomfortable the original Mini seats used to be? In 2001, for the new MINI, times had changed.
(David Wigmore)

5 Separation

BMW sells off the Rover Group

If a TV scriptwriter had offered up the summary of what happened to the Rover Group between late 1998 and mid-2000, his scenario would have been dismissed as far-fetched. Industrially, and financially, it made little sense and might not be believed. Yet the facts are now on record. The Rover Group, which had only been bought by BMW in 1994, was once again in crisis by 1998 – and was abruptly sold off in March 2000.

Mere words – BMW's own words – cannot do justice to what happened, for BMW's own Annual Report merely stated that: 'The Rover brand was not strong enough to perform the tasks intended for it. The measures which we have introduced to strengthen Rover's sales, dealer organisation and image have not led to the success we had hoped for. In addition, the general conditions for production in Britain, and thus for Rover, further deteriorated at the beginning of 2000.'

BMW, it seemed, was not ready to accept any of its own shortcomings, or those of the current (pre-BMW, that is) model range, and blamed everything on exchange rates: 'For example, the exchange rate for the British Pound against the German Mark was still some DM0.34 lower than it was at the end of 1999. Alone, this rise in the value of the British Pound in the interim has further increased the burden in the 1999 balance sheet by about DM1 billion ...' Presumably, it would have been politically incorrect to admit that it was the weakness of the new Euro, not the strength of Sterling, which had caused this shift?

Accordingly, in the same way that one might discard an old suit, BMW decided to shrug off Rover.

Before, during and after this crisis, the new MINI project carried bravely on. First of all, however, project responsibility would be taken back from the UK to Munich, then the project became a financial bargaining chip between the consortia trying to buy the Rover Group. Next there was the agony of deciding whether it should be assembled at Longbridge or Oxford (which was still known as Cowley by its workforce), and finally there was the *realpolitik* decision to let the launch slip by several months while the entire manufacturing facility was relocated.

A crisis of confidence

In 1998 and 1999, much of what happened in Birmingham swept over the head of the MINI project, which had already developed a massive momentum of its own. The R50/MINI was, after all, the largest single project currently taking shape at Longbridge, which was being extensively re-jigged to accept it. This meant that regiments of planners, builders, engineers and computer technicians were already 'heads-down' in making sure that they could bring the project into play, on time, and under budget.

Since 1997, the timing of this

From 1998 to 2000, BMW invested tens of millions into the Longbridge site, preparatory to building the new MINI there. This aerial shot shows West Works in the foreground, where the body shell was to be made, along with the conveyor which would take shells over the A38 road. Not yet built, in this shot, was the new MINI assembly hall, which was to be placed at the south-east (top right) of the complex.

86

programme had been agreed, firmed-up, and made known to every supplier, contractor and workman involved. Totally new body-in-white jigging, framing and welding – more robotised than any previous car which the Rover Group had ever built – were to go into West Works, and there would be a re-equipped and dedicated final assembly area in Longbridge's main East Works.

Kuka, of Augsburg in Germany, was the company chosen to design and install all the robots, whose performance was crucial to the success of this project. Starting in April 1998, they began placing machines in the newly-cleared facility in West Works in September 1999, and the entire line-up was completed in February 2000. This, as it turned out, was mere weeks before BMW's split from Rover was announced.

Body pressings would be transported into West Works from Swindon (where BMW owned a colossal, modern, pressings factory), from one of the German BMW factories at Dingolfing and from the re-equipped Land Rover complex at Solihull in Warwickshire. Engines would be shipped from Brazil, manual gearboxes would be manufactured at Longbridge itself, and (in due course) automatic transmissions would come from ZF at Friedrichshafen in Germany. Always assuming, of course, that there would still be a business in which to produce cars at all.

Late in 1998, BMW had concluded that the regeneration could only be assured if they moved in more German managers to ruthlessly operate a change round. Dr Hasselkus, they decided, could no longer cope with these problems, so he 'voluntarily' resigned in December of that year. Professor Werner Saemann replaced

Today's new cars have to be very strong to pass every crash test in the world's legislation. The new MINI was designed to be ultra-rigid, and was equipped with massive controlled-crush box-section 'chassis legs' located at each side of the engine bay.

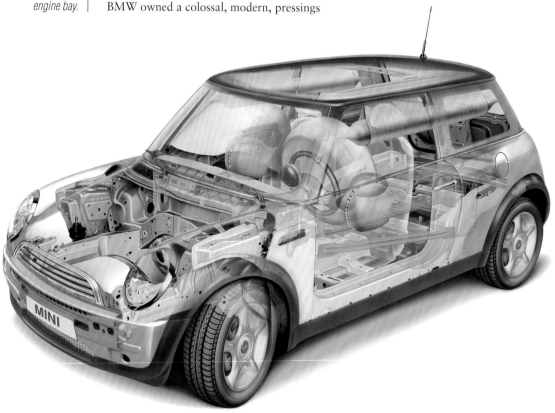

him, Christian John von Freyend moved in with him as Financial Director, and suddenly there were new (BMW) faces at all levels.

The financial key to this move was that although BMW had signed off the MINI project (in other words, had committed it to production at Longbridge), they wanted to offset the £400 million investment with grant aid from the British government to secure the future of Longbridge. £200 million had been requested. Approval was in the hands of Peter Mandelson, who was replaced at Christmas 1998 by Stephen Byers and no-one expected a quick and decisive response.

That, though, was not the end of the problem. Two of BMW's leading personalities – Bernd Pischetsrieder and Wolfgang Reitzle – had not only committed themselves to the Group turnaround, but to squabbling with each other. In the process they had made many enemies, so by February 1999 something approaching anarchy existed in Munich.

The outcome, at an all-day Board meeting held in Munich on 5 February 1999, was that Pischetsrieder resigned, and Reitzle (who had hoped to succeed him)

was also forced to resign. Pischetsrieder, it seems, had to go because the Rover Group had not been turned round under his chairmanship, while Reitzle was thought to be too flamboyant ('pushy' was one less complimentary word I have seen used), and did not appeal to BMW's financially ruling family, the Quandts.

In their place came the quiet man, the Board member who never spoke up first, but was considered to be very sound. He was Professor Dr Joachim Millberg, a one-time professor of engineering, who had only joined BMW in 1993.

For a time, with the business in turmoil, the atmosphere at Longbridge and Gaydon (to quote one insider) was described as: 'Every man for himself.' Even in 1998 BMW, looking for ways to improve Longbridge's productivity, had threatened to close the whole place if something was not achieved. From this moment on, BMW repeatedly put part of the blame on the high level of the British currency, stating that this made it difficult to contain costs, that Rover and Land Rover export models

Air bags are an essential part of any modern car's in-built safety equipment. On the new MINI, both driver and front-seat passenger were well protected, the bag specifications being up to the level of BMW 3-series models.

BMW
and the
Rover
Group

It was BMW's ownership of the Rover Group which led to the German company acquiring the MINI brand, for when the separation from the Rover Group followed in 2000, BMW retained those rights.

Originally, the first Mini was devised and put on sale by BMC in 1959, a company which became part of British

Leyland in 1968. Bankrupt in 1975, then rescued when the state took control, British Leyland was eventually broken up. Pieces (like Jaguar) were sold off, then the rump, retitled Rover Group in 1986, was finally sold off to British Aerospace in 1988, who promised not to strip any Group assets, nor to sell it off again for at least five years.

Throughout this traumatic period the classic Mini carried on in gradually-reducing production at the Longbridge (Birmingham) factory, while work on replacement models occasionally flared up, stuttered, but was inevitably cancelled.

Although BAe, it must be said, co-operated closely with the Japanese car-maker, Honda, and eventually

exchanged a minor equity partnership with them, it never invested enough commitment, capital, or management, to transform the Rover Group. In 1993/1994 the business was put on the market, and even though Honda was interested in taking a bigger share (but not taking over control), the whole business was sold off to BMW early in 1994.

BMW then set in train a major investment programme, which not only included new cars like the Land Rover Freelander (of 1998) and the Rover 75 (of 1998), and a massive new corporate engine plant at Hams Hall near Birmingham, but also a start to the new MINI project.

The rest, as they say, is history …

---

were costing too much and that inter-company trading was being unbalanced.

This was also the point at which BMW set up what they called a 'Turnaround Project Team', sending in cohorts of managers to all departments within Rover and Land Rover. Wolfgang Ziebart was the Product Development chief, while Dr Herbert Diess moved in on the manufacturing side. Before long there would be regular Airbus charter flights from Munich to Birmingham – one consequence being that many British managers began to feel marginalised and under-appreciated.

One of the first casualties was the MINI project team – not the MINI itself, but the team, its leaders and control of the product. As abruptly as responsibility for the project had been gifted to the Rover Group in May 1996, it was taken away again. Looking back, Chris Lee is still charitable about that upheaval: 'I was responsible for engineering the new MINI until early 1999, at which point it was decided that the project was becoming more and more German, with more and more German people working on it. BMW was taking more and more direct

control of the Rover business … At that point we were still on track for a start of production in September 2000.'

By the spring/summer of 1999, the evolution of the R50/MINI project was well on the way to completion. Following the premature viewing of a car in Frankfurt in 1997, Rover Group's fleets of test cars was regularly seen on the public highways without any camouflage. Chrysler 'Pentagon' engines, now delivered in some numbers, were finally performing up to specification, and supercharged Cooper engines were already producing the 163bhp which would be used on production cars in 2001/2002. BMW felt so confident about the MINI's future that they finally allowed a prototype to be seen at the massive Mini '40th Birthday Party' at Silverstone Circuit.

Not only that, but already there were persistent rumours that the German conversions specialists Alpina (who had already developed many other BMW-authorised cars) were to develop a 200bhp version of this car. Which explains, no doubt, why the engineering team had always been instructed to make space for the eventual use of 18in diameter road wheels …

Crash tests had already been carried out. After first analysing frame-by-frame 3D computer simulations to predict where problems might occur in absorbing crash pulses, and then by hurling £200,000-worth of individually assembled prototypes into crash barriers at all manner of specified trajectories, it became clear that an NCAP '4-star' rating could be assured.

Characters like Chris Lee, Dave Upex, Brian Griffin and Dave Saddington now drop out, completely, from this story. All stayed on with different responsibilities – Upex and Saddington, for instance, both became directors of Land Rover in 2000, while Chris Lee and Brian Griffin not only headed up the teams which produced the Rover 25 and Rover 45 cars, but became enthusiastic members of the MG Rover Group operation which followed.

One of the major handovers came in the design and styling area. Although every major item in the initial range had been designed, approved and was well on its way to series production, in 1999 the Design studio at Gaydon was already working away on proposed derivatives, which were intended to flesh out the range in future years. On the latest BMW 3-Series, for instance, there were to be saloon, coupé, estate car (Touring), hatchback, convertible, M-Series and sports car types – and BMW had the same strategy in mind for MINI.

Ex-MINI designers who remained at Gaydon when the premises were sold off to Ford, as part of the Land Rover purchase deal, recall how BMW had already sponsored the start of work on several new versions of the car. One, an obvious one, was a square-back body style, which the British called 'Traveller' and BMW called 'Touring'. Another was a five-door car, and

When the MINI project was taken back from the UK, to Munich in Germany, Gert Hildebrand became the head of MINI design.

a third (and most exciting of all) was a convertible, or 'Speedster' type. The 'Woody' (Traveller) and Speedster projects would be well down the road towards approval when the project was finally taken back to Munich.

By the end of 1999 – with the Rover Group virtually submerged under a tidal wave of BMW management, and with every department now directly controlled from Germany ('The BMW people believe their processes will work here because they work in Germany. In the end they are probably right, but the cost in terms of both money and organisational resources will be enormous …') – the MINI was moving steadily towards launch.

Wave after wave of 'sneak' previews appeared in motoring magazines and newspaper supplements, and Cooper S development pushed ahead on schedule. More and more evidence of new MINI facilities began to appear at Longbridge. At this time, let me emphasise, and even though British Government launch aid had not then been agreed, BMW was still totally committed to producing hundreds of thousands of new MINIS at Longbridge, there being no thought of any alternative location for this project.

Dr Herbert Diess, who would go on to become Plant Director at Oxford (where the MINI finally went into production in 2001), arrived at Longbridge in June 1999 as Manufacturing Turnaround Project Manager, Rover, Birmingham: 'I was there for less than a year. We made lots of progress, but it was not enough.'

'Lots of progress', incidentally, meant that by early 2000 the MINI project was still on schedule, the totally new body-in-white facility had been installed and tested (never before have I seen such a forest of Kuka robots in one building!), and West Works was ready to start delivering body shells for 'pilot' production to commence.

Over the road, in the main Longbridge complex, the Rover Group was in the process of commissioning a brand new assembly hall, where MINIS – and only

MINIS – were to take shape.

BMW wanted to get this right, and to emphasise that MINI was now to be a separate brand – neither 'Rover', nor 'BMW', but a marque on its own – the décor of the new hall was to be unique. Design had already been invited to visit the new buildings at Longbridge, to advise on colour schemes for the interior of that plant: 'BMW was very keen to give it a unique MINI feel, in contrast to the Rover car production lines.'

The first pilot-build cars were due to be built in the spring, but this rather depended on the ability of the suppliers to deliver. Then, and later, BMW and the Rover Group were tight-lipped about this period, but it seems that there were massive quality concerns still unresolved.

At the time industry insiders, who will not be named, said: 'The development programme is chaotic. Parts don't fit, there are gaps all over the place and every time BMW checks the car's progress, it changes things.'

'We are still receiving parts from suppliers made on prototype tools, when they should have started with production tools a few months ago …'

Even so, workforce training and recruitment was already under way, and – as always claimed – Job One was due in September 2000, though it now looked likely to slip to the end of the year. The car would be launched at the Paris Show in October 2000, and deliveries would begin in the winter of 2000/2001.

Although the Rover Group's financial losses were still known to be horrendous, BMW had already spent billions on its future, not only at Longbridge, Oxford and Gaydon, but at the Land Rover factory at Solihull, south-east of the centre of Birmingham. Considerable integration had already taken place, and the brand-new, still-unfinished, engine factory at Hams Hall, east of Birmingham, was then intended to supply four-cylinder petrol engines to BMW, to Rover, to MG and to Land Rover.

At this time BMW still continued to give the confident impression that all would be well, that they knew how to make it well and that there was a great future for Longbridge, just over the next horizon. In January 2000, indeed, BMW brought many of their Board directors over to Longbridge to host a conference, where chairman Joachim Millberg pointed out the progress that was being made. Part of that day was a factory tour, with everyone being bussed around the Longbridge site to see where the new MINI machinery was being put in place.

Sell out

This raised many hopes, which were soon to be seen as false. Only weeks later, the much-forecast cataclysm erupted. Out of nowhere, it seemed, BMW had decided to dismantle the Rover Group.

But this was no sudden development. As far as the public and the workforce were concerned, the news might have come as a shock, yet BMW had been discussing it for some months. By the time the bald announcement went out to the world's media on 15 March 2000, BMW had already agreed to sell the Longbridge site to Alchemy Partners, a fast-talking, financially-astute but essentially asset-stripping venture capital concern.

The Land Rover business, meantime, was to be sold off to Ford, who would also buy the modern high-tech Gaydon Technical Centre and proving grounds. Currently this contained the Rover and some of the MINI design, development and test teams, but was destined to become Land Rover's corporate HQ. BMW intended to retain their Oxford factory (where Rover 75s were being made), and the massive Swindon steel pressings factory.

Alchemy Partners' chief executive, Jon

Even while BMW was deciding to sell off Rover (and, in particular, to rid itself of the Longbridge site), testing of the definitive MINI was under way all over the world. This German-registered Cooper is in full and final condition, without any disguise, even down to the correct badges.

Early in 2000, pilot production of the new MINIs was just getting started at Longbridge. Except for the optional wheels, this One version was typical of the entry-level cars. Compared with the Cooper, the One was less highly decorated, with a painted (instead of brightwork) front grille.

Moulton, immediately became a hate figure at Longbridge, for it soon became clear that he cared little for cars (nor knew much about them), only for profits, and was intent on getting rid of much of the factory, and most of its products.

The next few weeks would be crucial for the future of the new MINI, which immediately found itself a major bargaining chip – perhaps *the* most important of many – in this multi-million game of industrial poker. Would it go ahead on time? Would it go ahead at Longbridge? Would it be transferred to another site? Would it – and this was an awful prospect – be cancelled altogether?

For the MINI, this could not have come at a worse moment. Pilot production was just beginning, the timetable for the next few months was already set in stone and any delay would inevitably mean a delay in getting cars on to the market.

Alchemy Partners, it seems, was already well-known to BMW's controlling Quandt family, and had first made contact with BMW in October 1999. Preliminary discussions about BMW's intentions for Rover Group were followed by a firm offer to 'take Longbridge off their hands', and by early 2000 this request became serious. Yet it took weeks of further negotiation, presentations and sheer old-fashioned nagging, to force BMW to a decision.

Alchemy Partners, please note, was not about to pay money for Longbridge, for all this bargaining took shape on the basis of:

'How much will you pay us to take the business away?' BMW wanted out of the cash-haemorrhaging crisis, but did not want to be seen to lose face in the process.

This is not the place in which to wring out every financial detail of what happened in the weeks which followed, for this has been covered quite superbly in a book called *End of the Road*, written by Chris Brady and Andrew Lorenz and published by *Financial Times*/Prentice Hall. In summary, if ever there was a textbook way of *not* handling a business deal, this was it.

In summary, BMW originally agreed that Alchemy Partners should buy part of the Rover Group, and at almost the same time they agreed to sell off Land Rover to Ford. The Land Rover sale would provide the dowry in which the Rover business sale could be wrapped.

Except that it didn't all work out. Even while Alchemy Partners was going through that financially vital 'nit-picking' period called 'Due Diligence', the one-time Rover Group chief executive, John Towers, set up a rival consortium (which he named Phoenix), got some support from the hapless government minister, Stephen Byers, and put in a rival bid.

The workforce at Longbridge loved this, for there was one major difference between the two supplicants. Whereas Alchemy Partners (Jon Moulton) wanted to dump responsibility for the MINI on BMW and slim down Longbridge to a marginal MG-orientated operation (with huge job losses), Phoenix wanted to keep Longbridge going, and its workforce intact. That was the Good news. The Bad news, however, was that while Alchemy Partners was working through the Due Diligence process with great professionalism, BMW refused even to talk to John Towers and Phoenix!

Although development and proving of the new MINI had just about been completed, and the very first pilot-built body shells had begun to trickle out of Longbridge's West Works, the entire project had now become a pawn in a fast-changing high-finance poker game. This, as far as I can see, is how things changed in March and April 2000:

- In March 2000, when BMW agreed to sell Longbridge to Alchemy Partners, they proposed to retain the Classic Mini facility at Longbridge, and to build cars until the originally-planned end of production, which for some time had been forecast for the autumn of 2000.
- BMW, on the other hand, not only wanted to retain the new MINI brand, but was determined to dismantle every part of the modern facility which had just been installed at Longbridge, move it to the Oxford factory (which they intended to keep), reinstall it and start MINI production from there.
- At this point, Alchemy Partners stated that they intended to redevelop parts of Longbridge as a 'niche-product' factory, concentrating on the MG brand, and that they were happy to see MINI go out of the door.
- By the end of March, John Towers, who was then the Chief Executive of Concentric, the Birmingham-based engineering business, had been approached by Longbridge's union bosses (who were quite appalled by what Moulton's Alchemy Partners was proposing to do). A group of Rover dealers chimed in – and suddenly, in early April, a counter-bid, Project Phoenix, was tabled. Most important, Phoenix planned to retain all of Longbridge, and wanted to keep the new MINI. Nevertheless, on 6 April BMW's Dr Saemann told John Towers that BMW would keep the MINI project to itself.
- On 28 April, with sale contracts already being drawn up, Jon Moulton's Alchemy Partners concern suddenly abandoned its bid, citing several financial dilemmas which could not be resolved. Immediately, therefore, Phoenix stated that they wanted to buy the business.

  Once again, Phoenix asked if they could retain the new MINI, but this was

refused. Instead, BMW offered to swap facilities with the Rover 75 project – Phoenix could take over the Rover 75 facilities from Oxford, after which the MINI facilities would take their place! BMW intended to produce the first 30,000 MINIs in 2001, followed by the full 100,000 in 2002. Further expansion, it was hoped, would follow.

- It might just work. On the basis that BMW would hand over a huge sum of money – £500 million [$725 million at 2000 exchange rates] was mentioned – Phoenix would buy the Longbridge complex for a mere £10 [$14.50], and hopefully keep the workforce intact.

The deal was finally done on 9 May 2000. The Phoenix consortium became Techtronic (2000) Ltd, the operating company would shortly become known as the MG Rover Group and the MINI link came to an end.

But not quite yet. The original-shape Classic Mini pottered on throughout this upheaval. 41 years and 5.3 million cars since the original Mini was launched in 1959, the pop star Lulu drove the very last model off the assembly lines at Longbridge on 4 October 2000.

Behind the scenes, and all the publicity razzmatazz, however, there was great sorrow at Longbridge. All signs of the new MINI, and its tenuous hold on life in this long-established Austin factory, had gone. Now it was about to be born, all over again, at Oxford. Was this a leap too far?

Would the new MINI have transformed the commercial fortunes of Rover's Longbridge plant? The consortiums bidding to take over from BMW thought so – but BMW was determined to retain its brand, and would soon move the production facility to Oxford.

95

6 All change at Oxford

The MINI's new home

The fight to move the new MINI production lines began the day after BMW finally sold the old Longbridge site to John Towers's Phoenix Consortium. It was a fight against every practicality – and a fight against time.

Theoretically, at that moment BMW could have elected to assemble the MINI in an overseas plant, but this was never practical. For one thing, BMW always looked on the MINI as a British car, not a European car – and for another, every one of BMW's existing German plants was already bursting at the seams.

This was a 'first' for BMW, the mighty German car-maker, for they had never before attempted anything like this. Practically, and functionally, it could certainly be done, but at a terrible price. The launch of the MINI would have to be delayed – that was obvious from the outset.

Before the separation, Longbridge, after all, had already started making pilot-production body shells. Everything would now come to a halt until all the high-tech new tooling and assembly facilities had been broken down, uprooted, transported to Oxford, re-assembled, tested and started producing bodies all over again. As many as 229 robots had already been placed at Longbridge – now they, and their computer-control technology, would have to be uprooted. The clock was ticking – and money was already beginning to flow out of the door.

Drive along Oxford's eastern by-pass today,

and you will skirt Cowley, which is a large suburb of the cathedral city of Oxford. Cowley, until the last century only a village quite separate from Oxford itself, gave its name to the original Morris Motors factory which grew up in the 1920s and made that village famous.

The factory on the east side of the dual carriageway, now known as BMW-Oxford, is the home of the new MINI. The front gate, complete with its BMW logos and corporate lettering, is impressive enough, but behind it the factory complex looks rambling and old.

But that is only the facade. On the inside, there are bright lights, smart colours, state-of-the-art assembly lines and a uniformly-dressed workforce. Starting from the arrival of steel pressings to be welded to others in the underpan assembly, MINIs gradually take shape on lines which are most impressively populated by robots. Except that the actual buildings are neither as modern, nor as glossy, as a European BMW complex in Munich or Steyr, this is a facility of which BMW is proud.

But it wasn't always like that. Here is a factory which grew from more modest beginnings as a body plant in the 1920s, a factory which was once umbilically connected to an even bigger plant on the other side of the by-pass, and one which *always* seemed to be too small for what it was asked to do.

Not only that, but here was a plant which started life as an independent

By the time the Oxford plant had been modernised, a forest of Kuka robots was ready to start building an endless stream of MINI body shells. This was just the first stage in a complete motor car manufacturing process. Note the massive crush tubes stretching forward from the bulkhead, along each side of the engine bay.

Before BMW could start rejigging the Oxford site in 2000, to make way for MINI assembly, the Rover 75 facilities had to be dismantled. After that the 75 saloon (right) and the estate car version which followed, were assembled at the MG-Rover factory at Longbridge.

business, suffered its first takeover in 1965, operated under several different managements until the 1980s and did not build its first complete car until 1992. The fact that the MINI is now built here, to high standards, and in big numbers, is little short of a miracle.

The fact that this factory – once known as the Pressed Steel Co. Ltd, and merely a builder of body shells – has survived, while the larger ex-Morris Motors, ex-BMC, ex-British Leyland, ex-Rover Group complex on the western side of the by-pass has been totally demolished, really is a miracle.

Credit for huge expansion in the 1950s – and the linking of Pressed Steel to 'Morris Motors' by an overhead conveyor – goes to the British Motor Corporation (and way back, of course, there is Mini DNA in that company), while blame for the destruction of the 'Cowley North' and 'Cowley South' factories is laid at the feet of British Aerospace, who owned Rover Group before BMW, and whose property arm (Arlington Securities) could see profit in razing old buildings and throwing up new ones for light industrial use.

Motor cars have been important to this south-eastern corner of Oxford for nearly 90 years. Yet, though the automotive history has been continuous since 1913, the story is very convoluted indeed. Not only have the cars been built atop several different patches of Oxfordshire soil, but their names have changed as well.

Time, then, for a short history lesson.

In the beginning there was 'Morris Cowley' where Morris cars were erected, and from the late 1920s an independent concern, the Pressed Steel Co. Ltd, grew up two hundred yards from it, to supply Morris and other car-makers with body shells. It was on this 'Pressed Steel' factory site that the BMW MINI factory would eventually take shape.

But not for many years. First of all the Morris factory gradually expanded to the south east, becoming barely separated from Pressed Steel only by a newly-built road. Then, in the 1950s, Morris became BMC, BMC threw up a new factory across the public road, to the south of the Morris Motors buildings, and body shells came to be delivered to both premises by enclosed overhead conveyors. In later years, planners estimated that the overhead conveyors held up to 300 body shells in limbo while they were crawling slowly from plant to plant. Incidentally, no fewer than 602,817 Classic Minis were produced here – though, of course, the vast majority of all Minis were made at Longbridge.

Soon after this, the road separating BMC from Pressed Steel was upgraded to dual carriageway (divided highway) status, and the web was finally spun. Then the corporate reshuffling (and financial traumas) began. BMC fell into British Leyland, which became BL under Government control, then the Austin-Rover business appeared and finally the Rover Group emerged. British Aerospace then bought Rover in 1988, set up even closer links with Honda (who bought a financial stake) – yet they then sent in the bulldozers in 1991/1992.

Still with me? The late 1980s strategy (which took no account of human factors, merely the financial bottom line) was to cut back on plant capacity, squeeze out costs and concentrate everything on to a smaller site. Three factories, separated by public roads, were to be reduced to one, which would be a complete assembly plant where the minimum of wasteful transportation would be involved. Steel panels would go in at one end of the complex, complete cars would roll out at the other.

It was only later that we realised just how much down-sizing was involved, for an existing complex of 900,000 square metres was to be drastically reduced. There would be a single 360,000 square metre car assembly hall, by which time the workforce was expected to stabilise at 3,000. Planned capacity would be 110,000 Rovers a year. The entire area used would shrink from 222 acres/90 hectares to 112 acres/46 hectares.

But which to close and which to develop? It was quite an easy decision, for Cowley South was too small, and Cowley North was both rambling and old-fashioned. What most historians still call the 'Pressed Steel' plant was therefore chosen for redevelopment and modernisation.

But it took years. First of all, in 1989, British Aerospace announced that it was to spend £130 million to regenerate the Cowley complex (what was not spelt out was that much of that capital would come from the property redevelopment of flattened factories …), and perhaps £450 million more on the new Rover models which would fill it.

All the building-up, as opposed to the knocking down, was to be concentrated on the vast body plant. What would be the assembly hall had been the original, massive, pressings building, and from the 1960s had become a body-in-white assembly shop. From 1992, for the first

Dr Herbert Diess directed the complete re-equipping of the Oxford plant, to make the new Mini, then stayed on as Plant Director.

time, it would begin to manufacture complete cars – Rover 800s, later Rover 600s and (from 1998/1999) Rover 75s. This was claimed to be a much more efficient building than those which were to be demolished in North and South works.

Initially, the Cowley North Plant (which was only assembling the sizeable Honda-Legend-based Rover 800 saloons) was readied for closure in 1991/1992, for the strategy was that a much-revised 'Mk II' version of the 800 would be assembled in the rejuvenated Body Plant.

The announcement that the Cowley South plant (which assembled Maestro and Montego models) was to be run down with the loss of 1,000 jobs, came in July 1990, for those cars were due to die in 1993: the rate of job losses was increased in 1991.

Rover Group, as it still was, proudly unveiled the new integrated assembly plant in July 1992, pointing out that all pressing, welding, painting and assembly operations were now to be carried out in this 'large car' assembly factory. Body shells for Rover cars now took shape in a building once allocated to building Rolls-Royce Silver Shadow monocoques! The investment involved, incidentally, had continued to increase, with more than £200 million already spent by this stage.

BMW take over

When BMW absorbed the Rover Group in 1994, therefore, they inherited a much-modernised Cowley complex, which was in great contrast to the rambling, ageing, Longbridge site. For years, it then seemed, BMW was happy to go along with assembly strategies which had already been laid down – which were that the smaller front-wheel-drive cars (Classic Mini, Rover 100, 200 and 400) would be built at Longbridge, and the larger cars (Rover 600 and 800) at Cowley.

And so, until March 2000 and the acrimonious hiving off of the Rover Group to the Phoenix Consortium, it remained.

At Cowley (which I must, henceforth, call BMW-Oxford), BMW then committed much new capital to the launch of the BMW-funded Rover 75, a car which took over from the 600 and 800 types, which was previewed in October 1998 and which went on volume sale in May 1999.

Then came the crisis of March 2000 when, as already detailed in the previous chapter, BMW finally lost all hope of turning the Rover Group into a business which would match up to its own standards. But, as already detailed, this was no clinical, business-school disposal.

If the business had been acquired by Alchemy Partners, the original consortium favoured by BMW to take over the Longbridge site and the Rover and MG marque activities, things might have been different, but it was John Towers's Phoenix Consortium who did the final deal, while BMW decided to keep the MINI brand.

In the reshuffle which followed, Phoenix agreed to take over the manufacture of still-new Rover 75s – but at Longbridge – while BMW decided that the new MINI (for which brand new assembly production facilities had already been installed at Longbridge) should be produced at Oxford!

Pandemonium! Those who did not realise the complexities of producing cars by computer and robot-assisted methods, could not see what the fuss was all about, but others with much experience of the world's motor industry blanched, crossed themselves and were relieved to be able to watch, rather than participate.

Immediately after the decision to sell off Longbridge was announced, BMW made it clear that it would keep the MINI brand, and that to do this it intended to move MINI assembly facilities to Oxford. To do so, a new company, BMW (UK) Manufacturing Ltd, was established in April 2000. Because BMW-Oxford was already busy building Rover 75s (a model which was to be continued – but at Longbridge!), this would be a major challenge.

Dr Herbert Diess, appointed as Plant Director at Oxford in May 2000, was at

the sharp end. Dr Diess, in fact, could already see both sides of the fast-evolving problem, for he had been Manufacturing Turnaround Project Manager at Longbridge from June 1999, then Plant Director at Longbridge from January 2000. Shepherding of the entire MINI project – jigging, framing, process control, and expertise, every nut, every bolt and every line of computer codes – could not have been in more expert hands.

'We had already started to make the first bodies in Birmingham,' Dr Diess told me, 'and we had the new building set up for the assembly plant – a new building – and then the decision was made. STOP! We had produced maybe the first 15 or 20 bodies at Longbridge when the decision was made to move the project. In my opinion, at that point we were at least six to eight months to go before "product maturity", when the facilities would be settled down. At first, I must say, at the beginning I did not like this very much but, looking back, I have to say that it was absolutely right, to make it clear cut. Not only is it right for BMW to build the MINI for itself, but it now gives

Longbridge a much better future and perspective.

'So, how could we do this? No-one at BMW had ever done anything like this before … I think this was unique for the motor industry, for we had to move two plants – an entire body-in-white facility and assembly line for the MINI 70 miles to the south, and we also had to move the Rover 75 in the other direction. We had to swap total facilities.'

For nine months – the rest of 2000 and early 2001 – the result was that nothing was being built at Oxford. Not even the appliance of technology, huge sums of money, or resolve, could reduce this further. Even though BMW would spend another £230 million on the changeover, to modernise and re-equip Oxford, some, but not all, of this nine months would be lost to delay the arrival of the MINI into the showrooms. BMW later claimed that only the Millennium Dome had exceed this as a construction project. The paint shop alone, they said, had cost £80 million when prepared for the Rover 75 in 1997.

'First of all we had to produce

Looking through history – in the 1930s Morris Motors built cars in Cowley (this is the complex closest to the camera) while Pressed Steel (separate block, at the top of the frame) built body shells for the industry. By the late1960s the plants would be vastly enlarged, and would be linked, with a by-pass road running through the plant (left to right in the picture). By the time the MINI arrived, the old 'Morris Motors' factory had been demolished, and that 'Pressed Steel' block had been submerged into a completely modernised assembly hall.

Cowley
heritage

Although BMW invested mega-millions into modernising and re-equipping the Oxford factory to produce the new MINI, the site, and some of the buildings, have a long history. What is now called BMW-Oxford, where final assembly of the MINI takes place, built its first body shells 75 years ago!

Its birth dates back to 1925, after British motor industry tycoon William Morris had visited the USA to study latest car-making trends. Becoming convinced that all-steel bodies were needed for future mass-production cars, Morris returned, got together with the Edward G. Budd Manufacturing Co., and set up The Pressed Steel Co. of GB Ltd on a greenfield site next to the Morris Motors factory, beyond the south-eastern edge of Oxford.

The first bodies were delivered to Morris in 1927, bodies for other makes of car followed in the 1930s, with the PSCo soon becoming Britain's largest independent body-making concern.

By the 1950s, Pressed Steel was supplying shells and body-chassis units to companies as diverse as Morris, Hillman, Humber, Rover, Standard-Triumph, Ford and Rolls-Royce. Business was so brisk that another PSCo factory (at Swindon) had to be developed to cope with the demand.

By that time the original factory had grown out of all recognition, eventually occupying more ground space than the Morris (later BMC)

assembly plant which was 'next door', and to which it became linked by an overhead conveyor.

Bought out by BMC in 1965, and becoming an integral part of British Leyland from 1968, this business eventually concentrated on supplying the parent company, and its name changed several times. The final upheaval came early in the 1990s (before BMW took control), a point at which the old Morris Motors/British Leyland car assembly factories were closed down, demolished and redeveloped; at the same time the adjacent historic 'Pressed Steel' plant was completely rejigged to manufacture complete motor cars.

First the Rover 600 and 800 types, plus the MG R-V8 sports car then – briefly – the Rover 75 model, and then the new MINI have all been built there.

Work gets under way at BMW Oxford on the welding together of the complex steel body shell of the new MINI. Note the complete absence of human beings in shot – for the production of such shells is now a highly-automated business, computer controlled, laser-sensed and programmed from a remote terminal. In future years, this welding line will be able to deal with several different body variants.

additional Rover 75s, over and above the schedule – about 2,600 complete cars, including many diesel-engined types, which they were short of – because there would otherwise be a gap in MG Rover's stocks of cars to sell: the last of those cars was built on 5 July 2000. Then we had to build an extra number of unpainted bodies – I think it was 6,700 shells – which Longbridge could use to build up their own Rover 75 production cars while the existing body-in-white facilities were being re-installed.

'Then we had to strip out the whole body-in-white facility at Oxford, where a £100 million investment made for the Rover 75 had to be dismantled, identified, put on to trucks and moved to Longbridge.'

But, where to store those shells? Not at Oxford, of course, where the contractors were just about to arrive. Fortunately there was an ideal place, at Longbridge, which was new, bright, but empty – the hall which had just been prepared to accommodate MINI assembly!

Some good, therefore, came out of disaster at Longbridge, though by the end

of 2001 that hall had still not been brought into use for anything other than storage.

'Next,' Dr Diess recalled, 'we had to start by reshaping the building areas. Because there was going to be a different way of building the shells, we needed pits and access in different areas, and we needed to make allowances for future versions that I can't tell you about.'

Nothing is more depressing than the sight of a famous, important, industrial site being levelled in the interests of progress. Bulldozers are no respecters of reputation, or of sentiment, for their blades plough heedlessly through walls which have enclosed legendary products in the past. For a time, at Oxford, there was more devastation than rebirth. But things were about to look up.

This was the time, incidentally, when entire redundant buildings were flattened by the bulldozers in an effort to remove otherwise space-wasting empty blocks which were no longer needed, and to make way for what would surely follow in the early 2000s. Even at the end of 2001, for

At this stage in MINI assembly, the painted shell is being carried on slings which place the body on its side, so that the workforce can add pieces to the underside without having to bend down, or crawl underneath. The rear suspension assembly has already been added, but 'body drop' (on to the engine/transmission assembly) is yet to come.

instance, the massive factory buildings (old, but extensively modernised in the 1990s) which had been used to assemble Rover 600 body shells were still being razed.

'We had to clean up the whole area,' Dr Diess told me, 'and this started on the same day that we ceased production of Rover 75s. As the last 75 moved through the factory, the contractors followed it. We needed to change a lot of the plant, for the MINI was going to take up more space than the 75 had done. This was because the MINI was to be built in the BMW way. The body-in-white facility involved the manufacture of every sub-assembly. But we never considered doing our own press work here. We have the Swindon press shop [this was originally a satellite 'Pressed Steel' factory, which is only 30 miles from Oxford, the two buildings being connected by road and rail], which is very modern.

We also receive outer skin parts and major structural parts from Land Rover at Solihull.'

Until the autumn of 2000, the Oxford factory was the home of BMW planners and factory construction specialists, the bulldozers, the diggers and the men with the hard hats – but not of a workforce assembling cars; although 300 people were fully occupied seeing that every scrap of Rover 75 production equipment moved north, and then readied themselves to see MINI move south. Then the entire assembly force either had to be found something else to do, or be temporarily laid off, or be re-trained, or spend time working in other BMW factories. About 300 people went to Germany for a time, and up to 100 went to the Spartanburg factory in the USA, where Z3 sports cars and X5 4x4s were being made. In any case, the

104

workforce took an extended, nine-week, summer break.

By September 2000 the body-in-white facilities for the new MINI were going into place at Oxford, but it would be January 2001 before the first few pre-production cars were built, and well on into the spring – April 2001 was the forecast – before true volume production could start. All in all, the new-new Oxford plant would be able to produce up to 100,000 MINIs a year (more when a three-shift operation was introduced), with the limit of capacity constrained by the paint shop.

This was when the rehiring and redeployment of the manufacturing workforce began – in true flow-line methods first for the body shop, then for the paint shop and finally for the assembly hall. By the time the MINI was in full production in the autumn of 2001, and

when 300 cars (soon to be increased to 500) were being built every day, 4,300 people of all types would be employed at Oxford, more than 2,500 being full time 'associates', and others being on contract or less permanent duty. Only 100 of them originally came in from BMW in Germany, though that figure was more than doubled when the re-equipped factory was being fired up, and all its systems (particularly computer systems) were being installed.

This, too, was a time when there was intense negotiation between BMW and its trade union organisers, to achieve a totally flexible arrangement of staffing and working. Although up to 500 'Rover 75' employees had decided to take early retirement after receiving a very valuable 'package', every other employee was once again offered a job on the new MINI. Union agreements, far too complex to

Towards the end of MINI assembly, the almost-complete cars are carried down from an overhead area to ground level, where wheels are positioned and bolted into place by a multi-axis tool. From that moment, the MINI is on its own wheels and almost ready to roll. Please note – every operative carried his name on his overalls.

After being assembled, every Mini is thoroughly checked over, especially to make sure that engine exhaust emissions are within specified limits.

detail here, finally secured great flexibility: 'We wanted to cut off the Rover Group history, the old Rover Group agreement which was not according to the BMW philosophy. We needed more flexibility, and more labour capacity when the market demand is there.'

Early in 2001, when the job was finally done, BMW-Oxford had been re-created, as a Mini-only assembly plant able to build one car every 100 seconds. In the beginning the ultimate capacity was limited by what the paint shop could handle. Once volume production began in April – first at 25 cars a day, then 100, and (by mid-summer) 300 – the workforce expanded to suit.

'The whole investment in the plant is based around that cycle time, Dr Diess told me. 'But my experience is that you must always follow a careful "ramp-up" curve, because it's not only what we have to do in our own plant, but how we prepare our suppliers – they all have to follow the same rate of climb, they have to hire people, and they have to train people. It's always the

same – there was nothing new with this project.' That careful ramp-up involved the phased delivery of two important 'building blocks' – the engine and the gearbox. Both had their own particular 'pipelines' to establish.

Production of the 'Pentagon' engine at Tritec Motors Ltda, at Campo Largo, near Curitiba, in Brazil, began in series in mid-2000, though the first engine of all had been completed as early as September 1999.

The economic case for building engines in Brazil was quite conclusive – other European-based car makers also have production facilities in the same coastal region of Brazil – but the transportation problem needed thought.

From Curitiba to Oxford – consider the challenge. Once the engines had been manufactured, they had to be crated – 80 at a time – then loaded into containers and hoisted on board ship to spend six weeks at sea on the way to the UK. At any one time, BMW estimates, up to 20,000 'Pentagon' engines (one fifth of annual

MINI output) are en route from one factory to the other.

Then, once the containers had been unpacked at Oxford, every engine had to travel down what is known as the 'Engine Dress' line, where the European-sourced ancillaries (which were not sent to Brazil for fitment) were bolted into place, and where the engine was then mated with its transmission.

The manual gearbox, as detailed in Chapter 3, was a modified version of that already being used in the small MG Rover products, generically known as the R65, but in detail was claimed to be a much better gearbox than it had been in earlier years. Manufacture – gear cutting, assembly and pre-delivery testing – was carried out at the Cofton Hackett factory (the same factory, just a short step down the road from the main Longbridge East Works complex which also made engines).

In the original scheme of things, the gearboxes would have been an 'in-house' product, but since the separation of BMW from Rover Group, the Cofton Hackett site has been split, with engine production controlled by MG Rover Group, and with a new BMW-owned business, Midland Powertrain, manufacturing transmissions.

The original intention was that they would merely have been trucked a few hundred yards up the road but, following the relocation of the MINI facility to Oxford, they had to be transported down the busy M40 motorway which linked it to Longbridge. Once again, with 300–500 transmissions to be manufactured every day, a sizeable number of them would always be in transit. Today's 'just in time' philosophy of making cars, where factory-held stocks are kept to a minimum, meant that any delays could soon become a serious concern.

Although the MINI Cooper got most of the glamour in the opening months of production, it was the 90bhp MINI One which was the most frequently sold 'entry level' type. Although British One prices started at £10,300, many of the cars were loaded up with optional extras from the big list already offered by BMW.

What if bad weather closed the M40? Snow – yes, even in temperate Britain, it has done this in the past – might block off the way: 'We like to keep our stocks down, but we can usually carry on making MINIS for up to two days before we completely run out.'

Marking time? No time

In the meantime the MINI engineering project team, once again led by Dr Heinrich Petra, was completing the development of the new MINI, and the purchasing side was building up the framework of all its suppliers.

'Of course the production schedule slipped because of the move from Longbridge to Oxford,' Dr Petra admits, 'but that did not affect us. We had to finalise the handling. We would make no compromises, and because the centre of gravity of the MINI is so low, we could make it feel like a go-kart. You could get into a MINI without being told what it was and, as soon as you saw it, you would say:

When the original, and much-loved, Mini-Cooper was on sale in the 1960s, no more than 15,000 such cars were ever built in a year. At Oxford, annual output of MINI Coopers is expected to be at least twice that level.

"That's a MINI." Then, when you drove it, you would know that it was. We always used the old Mini as a target for the handling – not for the ride, of course, but for the handling. No-one else had ever got handling, and steering, like that – and we wanted to keep it.'

By the end of 2000 Rover, then BMW, had tested the MINI all over the world. Much basic work was done in Europe, at the Gaydon Proving Ground in Warwickshire and at BMW's massive test track at Miramar in the south of France. Then, as Dr Petra reminded me, for ultra-cold winter testing they made the pilgrimage to Sweden and Finland, for very hot climate conditions they visited Dubai and then it was thought advisable to go to South Africa, to North America and to Japan. Because of their wide vehicle range, and their important sales in those markets, BMW have permanent, secure, testing facilities in Japan and in North America. And, of course, when visiting Tritec Motors in Brazil, to try the cars in

the hot and humid conditions of the rain forests of Brazil …

Total test mileage? Several millions, of course – certainly too many to count.

Dr Petra and other top BMW managers, incidentally, dismissed any comparison with best-selling cars like the VW Golf ('Boring cars, not at all the same as the MINI.') Incidentally, Dr Petra, who still visits Oxford every week, flying in and out on scheduled airlines from Munich, told me how much he had learned by hiring different cars at Heathrow: 'It is very interesting. I am an ordinary customer. This week it was a Peugeot 206!'

Yet there were problems – not insuperable, but significant. In the spring of 2000, newspaper reports began to talk about the unacceptable quality of some of the 'off-tools' components which were arriving from outside suppliers. In the past, maybe, Rover would have had to accept a supplier's idea of acceptable quality – but not BMW. That was then, and this … was progress. Those whose pieces fell short were firmly told to go back and try again … and again … and again if necessary.

By the end of 2000, the reborn Oxford factory, still looking a bit bruised on the outside, but virtually brand-new inside, was ready to come to life once again. Even though trucks full of new factory material would still arrive every few minutes, and trucks of spoil, scrap or redundant equipment would be leaving at the same time, Oxford was once again open for business. Old buildings were being flattened, usable buildings were being refaced and given a real makeover, and dereliction was giving way to landscaped surroundings.

An old complex reborn? Of course – but only you and I need know that, for once inside the door, this was BMW's idea of what a state-of-the-art car assembly plant should look like.

'A factory is never finished,' Dr Diess told me, with a wry smile, 'and we must provide options for the future, for enlargement. We also had to reduce the overall cost of running the site, and – yes, this is important – we had to make it look a lot nicer. We needed to reach the same levels of productivity and quality as we would get from a new greenfield site. We could still add more buildings if we wanted. The whole site is 850,000 square metres [which means that only half of it is built over], the right size for building 100,000 to 200,000 cars every year. But the tidy-up business will be 80 per cent finished by the end of 2001, and we will be in good shape by the end of 2002.'

In spite of all the disruption caused by the move from Longbridge to Oxford, BMW is proud that the delay was kept down to such a low level. Dr Diess points out that the MINI was shown to its public in the autumn of 2000 – at the Paris Show, where its launch had been pencilled in many months before the upheaval took place. Although this was not admitted early in 2000, it was already clear that Longbridge could not start building acceptable-quality production cars until the start of 2001, and that sales could not possibly have begun until the spring of that year: 'Yes, there was a delay. Of course there was. But it wasn't much. We kept it down to three months, no more. We actually built our first production car on 26 April 2001 …'

[On a matter of motoring history, no-one seems to have picked up one startling fact – that the new MINI went into volume production almost exactly 500 months after the first-ever Issigonis Minis were assembled …]

By the spring of 2001, however, it was almost too late to have second thoughts, or to make changes. Pilot-build, then pre-production, MINIs had been rolling steadily off the virgin fresh assembly lines at Oxford since the beginning of the year, and the very first true production cars were produced on 26 April. The marketing effort to prepare the public for the new model had been rolling since 2000.

Would the new MINI be a success? Now BMW was about to find out.

109

7 MINI
on sale

From the summer of 2000, marketing activity for the new MINI went into overdrive. After years of admitting that they were to produce a new MINI, BMW now had to convince its clientele that the wait had been worthwhile.

Strategies as big as this need to be simple and effective – with the main points to be repeated time and time again. Right from the start, therefore, BMW wanted the world to know that this was not just another new car, but the rebirth of a legend. Not only was this the first proper replacement for the 41-year-old Mini, but it was a MINI – no more and no less. The new car wasn't a Mini, it wasn't a Rover Mini, it wasn't even a BMW Mini – but it was a MINI.

Appointed to direct the marketing launch of the new car, Torsten Muller-Oetvoes knew that he had to handle a very precious cargo: 'We had to look carefully at the history of the Mini, what it stood for, and what a Mini really was. We had decided that the new MINI could not be a visual "fake", or lookalike, of the older car, so we looked at the car in terms of driving fun, and in terms of a "go-kart" feel – all those handling aspects which had made the old Mini so famous.'

Crucially – and this point has already been made – BMW decided that the MINI should develop its own brand, which was something not attempted with the earlier car. To add the famous BMW name and 'spinner' badge to the MINI was thought to be confusing – and, in fact, BMW's directors did not want to see their precious blue-and-white symbol pushed so far down the size scale. The car was, in fact, to become a brand within a brand, with separate managers and departments looking after the entire project. In the mid-2000s, too, BMW was hoping to do the same with their first-ever Rolls-Royce: 'BMW knew very precisely how to build a premium car, but our clear intention with MINI was not to develop a premium brand. From the beginning, as 40 years ago, it was to be a car affordable by everybody, a small-engined family car. We do see a big potential for the MINI brand, and that there is a real chance to capitalise on it. We have made a big investment in the brand, necessary because of what we thought, long term, about what we could do with the brand. There is a long-term strategy behind the whole thing.'

But was the MINI to be marketed as a British car, a German car, or as a European car? The answer – and I should have seen it coming – was that it was to be sold as a 'world' car, for sale in every important world market, and idealised for all of them: In two or three years' time, they hoped, people would even forget where it is being made ...'

Part of the huge investment, the huge belief, in the future of the brand came during 2000, when the big push towards launch began in the early autumn. Cleverly looking for the sympathy vote, but in an

BMW's options list for the MINI is full of high-tech 'toys', including satellite navigation. With sat-nav installed, the speedometer is relocated to a pod behind the steering wheel.

understated fashion: 'We've had to sell off Rover, but we kept MINI because we believe in it. We've had to move it to another factory, and we can't start to deliver before 2001, but here's a preview …' – BMW then unveiled the car, officially, at the Paris Salon in September/October 2000. In spite of all the engineering, financial and practical traumas of the previous five years, the car had come into public view on time, at the very occasion planned for it in 1997.

It was at this point, of course, that all the rumours were laid to rest, some being confirmed, and some being written off completely. There would indeed be a basic model (to be called 'One') and a Cooper, and they would have different levels of power output, but there was no sign of the smaller (1.4-litre) engine which had been rumoured for so long.

This, too, was the first time that BMW had ever published any dimensions for their new car, so although many of us had known for some time that the MINI was going to be so much larger than the Classic

Mini, none of us had quite realised by how much. Here was a new car which was not only 12 per cent longer, and 265 per cent more powerful, but it was also 66 per cent heavier, and took up something like 45 per cent more volume than before. Not so mini any more, perhaps? Maybe so, but it was best not to mention that in front of a MINI marketing man.

Surprisingly, the launch ceremony in Paris was not at all exciting. Minis, after all, had always been about fun, glamour, pizzazz and sheer cheeky joie de vivre – but not this time. When unveiling the MINI, BMW made much of all the virtues which I have already rehearsed so thoroughly – there being much emphasis on branding, on rebirth and on technical virtues, but this was somehow subdued behind the inherent seriousness of the occasion.

Maybe it was because we had all been waiting for this moment for so long, maybe there was an element of déjà vu about the occasion – and maybe it was because almost every detail of the new cars had been trailed (officially, or unofficially) well

in advance. The only surprise was that BMW admitted that they were already considering the development of other types – coupés, convertibles and estate car (Touring) versions all being mentioned. Computer simulations of possible shapes were shown, but nothing further was to be heard, or seen, of such cars for the next two years.

And, in spite of the long gestation of the project, MINIS were still not yet available to be driven. This, therefore, was the time to study BMW's marketing philosophy – there would be an entry-level 'One', and a more powerful 'Cooper'– and the way that the car was so obviously intended to be sold all over the world. In the UK, where world-wide sales would begin on 7 July 2001, entry-level prices would start at around £10,000 – which was far removed from the bargain-basement prices offered by some Far Eastern makers, but still a commercially attractive level. Significantly, cost over-runs which had been obvious in 1998/1999, when control of the project had been taken back from Britain to Germany,

had clearly been dealt with.

As far as the exterior style was concerned, there were absolutely no surprises – spy photographs, stretching back to 1997, had made sure of that. This, though, was the first time that we really saw how shallow the passenger cabin really looked – Rover Design had done a great job in refining Frank Stephenson's theme, and somehow the lowered roof line didn't harm the cabin space too much. We saw, also, how the bonnet would open – that the entire front-end sheet-metal was hinged at the bulkhead, and that the panel shut line between the bonnet pressing and main body replicated almost exactly the slope of the Classic Mini's exterior seams. Clever.

The fact that this shape harked back, in so many ways, to that of the original, was quite intentional, for BMW believe that its customers need to be able to rely on the shape and feel of a brand: 'If you look at any successful brand – like the Coca Cola bottle – you have to be very careful to make any new product close to the older one, not too far away.'

In the original Classic Minis, air conditioning was achieved by opening the windows, but in the new MINI there was a state-of-the-art installation built in to the bulkhead. In conditions like this – in Arizona – every technological aid was appreciated.

Size **matters?**

Size. That's the problem. To call this new car a MINI means that many people expect it to be a similar size to the original. But it isn't. Not by a long way. In fact, one comment made to me, purely as an aside, is that the new MINI occupied 45 per cent more volume than the original car.

Here, therefore, is a telling comparison between the new MINI and the original 1959 version:

Feature	Original Mini (1959)	New MINI (2001)
Overall length (in)	120.25	142.7
Wheelbase (in)	80.2	97.1
Width (in)	55.0 (No mirrors) 66.4 (across shell)	75.8 (Over the mirrors)
Height (in)	53.0	55.0
Front track (in)	47.4	57.5
Maximum cabin width (in)	46.0	52.0
Engine size/power (cc/bhp)	848/34 *or* 1275/63	1598/90 *or* 1598/114
Unladen weight (lb)	1,380 2,481	2,293 to

Compared with the old, therefore, the new MINI was a much larger car. It had a 21 per cent longer wheelbase, was 19 per cent longer overall, had an 88 per cent larger engine, was between 265 per cent and 335 per cent more powerful, and weighed between 66 per cent and 80 per cent more.

Clearly Alec Issigonis and BMW had different packaging ideas, for although the new car had a much better driving position, it had rather less space in the rear seats than the old. The modern car, though, was much better equipped.

MINI? Some people thought it should have been called MAXIMINI …

Wheels – 15in in diameter, even on the 'One' – were large, and looked it, and there was no doubt that the designers' intention to make this into a muscley little car had succeeded.

A wheel at each corner? Of course. Minimal front and rear overhang? Naturally. A flat, almost horizontal roof line? What else? A contrasting roof colour for the Cooper? Traditional, and continued. Yet, a simple car? Not at all.

Simple, maybe, in its basic exterior style, but once you opened the bonnet and peered into the engine bay, the sheer complexity of modern motor cars was obvious once again. A 16-valve engine, lots of piping, provision

Once the MINI went on sale in 2001, BMW was determined to talk up the trendy, forward-looking, youthful image of the new car. Its showroom designs, complete with scale models and accessories, were all part of this approach.

for air-conditioning, radiators, mysterious electronic black boxes, twin bonnet-holding-down latches, and much more – this was not the simple sort of car that Classic Mini enthusiasts could deal with.

The massive bonnet pressing, too, deserved study. Engineers told me that in the development phase one of their most difficult jobs was to stop it vibrating on its mountings (thus disturbing headlamp alignment), and agreed that this was one reason for two separate holding down latches.

The bonnet panel, I suggested, was one of the largest single pressings I have ever seen: 'Yes, and at the design/styling stage that gave us a real problem. In fact, the original shape, as signed off, wasn't really feasible in manufacturing terms, and we had to ask for it to be made slightly flatter – slightly less 'deep drawn' – than had originally been hoped.'

It was inside the car – when you looked at the fascia, and the tubular/contrast colour of the door furniture – that the

realisation of this as a trendy little car began to seep through. Original Minis had been simple and – yes – crudely built, with one central instrument, an open parcel shelf, stowage bins in the doors, sliding window frames and a heater that was both an optional extra and a joke.

On the new car, not only were high-performance features like power-assisted steering and four-wheel-disc brakes standard, even on the entry-level cars, but so were four airbags, anti-lock brakes, remote central locking, electric window lifts and a BMW security system. Air conditioning (approx. £500) and leather trim (about £600) were both to be optional.

The M<small>INI</small> for 2001, on the other hand, was as well-equipped as an entry-level 3-Series BMW (but this was not badged as a BMW, don't forget …), well furnished, and as trendy as the newest stereo or high-street shop. Satellite navigation would be an option – which put the M<small>INI</small> one-step ahead

Although M<small>INI</small> is a brand owned by BMW, there was no sign of BMW in the showroom displays and designs in 2001. M<small>INI</small> was being promoted heavily as a new brand of its own, and customers were encouraged to add their own touches to new cars. The optional wheels on the yellow M<small>INI</small> Cooper are a case in point.

115

of all of its potential rivals. Cup holders? Of course – for this car was always meant to be sold in the USA, where deliveries would begin in 2002.

Then there was the oh-so-trendy design of doors, different-coloured bars with which to pull, and the 'Hey Guys, I'm different' detailing. This certainly didn't impress everyone. As the much-respected British writer, Phil Llewellin, commented: 'There were puzzled looks when I asked a BMW engineer if the big bar that runs across the inside of each door concealed a side-impact beam. That would make sense.

In fact, what this fancy door-pull does best is make the stowage bins vastly less practical by dramatically reducing their capacity. That's stupid …'

And then there was the driving position. Here, for the first time, was a MINI where the driver was not going to need the service of a chiropractor before long, and where long arms were not necessary. BMC's Alec Issigonis once famously quipped that he liked his drivers to be uncomfortable so that they could stay alert – but not any more. BMW had started on the premise that the cabin should be comfortable, and

A red MINI Cooper, young people in the showroom and youth-market posters and displays on the walls – this was how BMW set out to establish its new MINI brand in the early months.

that the driver should feel as relaxed and well-supported as in a 3-Series. It was all that, and more, because even on the entry-level 'One' the rack-and-pinion steering had power assistance, while the four-wheel disc brakes were properly servo'd too.

Seeing the car up close, too, reminded us of just how much larger the new MINI was than the original had ever been – for its bulk was altogether more noticeable, particularly in the darker colours. Yet almost everyone seeing the car for the very first time seemed to be disappointed by the lack of rear seat space – and BMW soon got used to explaining that modern crash tests required more front-end crush space, that the MINI had a much more driver-friendly front-seat layout, and that (rather shamefacedly, perhaps) there were limits to what could be achieved with such a low roof line.

They were, on the other hand, not only proud of being the first user of this new Tritec Motors Ltda-made new engine, but also of the way that it gave the new car a sparkling performance. The MINI, let's make it clear, was in a completely different league from *any* of the old-type Minis which it replaced. The fastest of all the old types, for instance, had been the Mini-Cooper 1275S, which had always struggled to reach 100mph, whereas the new MINI Cooper should be a 125mph machine – and there would be much more performance to come from the still-rumoured (but not denied) MINI Cooper S.

Even after the MINI was shown off for the first time, much still remained to be revealed. An automatic transmission version was sure to follow, and it was known that it would be a CVT type (CVTs had been used in early BMW 'city car' project machines), but no more than that was published. In due course there would be a whole range of equipment and dress-up packs, but these would all have to wait for through-flow production to get under way at Oxford.

In the meantime, the marketing machine swung purposefully into action. Because

this was still seen as a British car, made in a British factory, BMW decided that the British home market should be the first to receive deliveries of the MINI. For the first few months, therefore, Oxford would concentrate on building right-hand-drive 'domestic' cars.

Advertising agencies will stop at nothing! In 2001 the subliminal message here is: 'I love my MINI Cooper so much that I could kiss it, all over …'

In the UK, waiting lists rapidly built up, though these were not expected to last beyond the end of 2001 (as assembly numbers built up), bargain-hunters immediately started looking around for ex-demonstration Coopers (they were invariably disappointed), and once the not-for-sale-until-2002 Cooper S was previewed, all manner of pushing and shoving took place to get to the front of order books.

Pragmatically, this was the best way to go ahead, for BMW would be able to keep a close eye on the first cars that entered service, and quickly deal with any small problems which occurred. Events proved that they were wise, for soon after launch, in August 2001, there was a reliability scare concerning the build up of static electricity in the fuel filler neck, and the potential of sparks causing a fire, but this was swiftly resolved by a recall and a quick 'fix'.

It also gave the suppliers a chance to settle into their rhythms. Although the largest single component – the engine – came from far-off Brazil, and the engine

alternator came from Denso in the USA, the majority of supplies came from the UK, and from Germany. At this point BMW was listing 119 suppliers (almost half of the total) as British, with 83 suppliers (37 per cent) being based in Germany. The balance was spread around Europe – 14 in France, eight in Italy, three each in Ireland and Austria, and just one each in Belgium and Hungary. No fewer than 2,415 different parts would be fitted to a MINI on the final assembly lines.

Like all the others, those single suppliers, incidentally, were vital to the make-up of the new car, for the fuel lines and vacuum lines came from Hungary, while it was the ZF transmission concern which would supply power-assisted steering and CVT automatic transmissions, partly from Belgium.

The supply jigsaw, in fact, was impressive. Moving in from first contact with the road, tyres came from the UK and Germany, wheels from Austria and Italy, brake discs from Spain, brake calipers from the UK and Germany, suspension arms

Waiting lists for the MINI Cooper built up rapidly before it went on sale in Britain in July 2001. Even in November, there were still many envious glances when we photographed this car. (David Wigmore)

came from Germany, springs and dampers from France and anti-roll bars from Germany. Then there was the rest of the running gear to be considered …

To those of us used to strolling up and down car assembly lines of the past, the Mini assembly hall at Oxford looked amazingly clean, brightly lit and uncluttered. The era of stacking pallets of parts alongside the tracks has long since disappeared, for on the Mini many parts appeared in slings from above at the right time, and in appropriate quantities.

Assembly, naturally, starts from a painted body shell which has been delivered from the adjoining paint shop, one of the more enduring mysteries being that the passenger doors were not in evidence until a late stage, when they reappeared, completely assembled with glass and trim, to be allocated to their original body shell.

Engines, in the meantime, were being 'dressed' (that quaint motor industry expression) and mated to their transmissions in a small area to one side of the lines, and when the time was ripe they

would be transferred, by computer-controlled conveyor, to the assembly line itself. Not at ground level, where human beings and traffic jams might ensue, but overhead, where the headroom was enormous.

BMW, clearly, wants its workforce (or 'associates', as they are called) to be as comfortable throughout their nine-and-a-quarter hour shift. At one stage in this modern process, each body shell is carried in a spit, on its side so that components can easily be added to the underside, and at others the shell is high (and ready to meet the engine/transmission pack and the rear suspension assemblies (which are offered up from underneath). And if anything unauthorised gets in the way? BMW try to ensure that it cannot, but there are cut-off devices to take care of that.

The entire fascia/dash/instrument panel – ready assembled, plumbed, trimmed and almost ready to go – is offered up through the empty door space (before the doors get back together with their shells). Only six hours earlier the supplier, Magna, had

No need for big badging on the new Mini, which is recognisable from every angle. The Cooper badge on the tailgate, though, tells everyone of the extra power in that model.
(David Wigmore)

Performance comparisons:
chalk and
cheese

The more I look into the new and the old, the more I wonder why BMW called its new car a Mini. In performance there is simply no comparison between new and old:

Statistic	New Mini Cooper 1598cc/114bhp	Original Mini Cooper 997cc/55bhp
Top speed (mph)	125	85
0–60mph (sec)	9.3	18.0
0–80mph (sec)	17.3	50.6
Standing 1/4-mile (sec)	17.4	20.9
Overall fuel consumption (Imperial mpg)	32.5	26.8
Unladen weight (lb)	2,481	1,435

Headlamps on, look out world, the Mini Cooper is coming. Once on sale, it captured its market at once. (David Wigmore)

started to build it up, in its own factory. In the glazing cell, all the glass is lifted from track side storage by sucker-equipped robot arms, and carefully lined up before being bonded into position.

The hard labour, and certainly the grime, of old times, is nowhere to be found.

The assembly tracks still move, of course, but the 'skillets' carrying each individual Mini are covered by polished wood. Maybe this is not a clinically clean environment, but there doesn't seem to be much mess – no wrapping paper on the floor, no empty cartons, and certainly no

cigarettes, for this is a smoke-free zone. Yet this is a mass-production installation, so the tracks creep inexorably forward, and the workforce needs to keep moving to maintain station. For one car, the total final assembly time is about five hours – and the cars keep on coming.

(BMC's Sir Leonard Lord, who inspired the birth of the original Mini, was a chain smoker, and would no doubt have been appalled by the latest wave of political correctness. But that was then, and this is – the twenty-first century.)

Spreading the word

In the meantime, BMW's formidable marketing machine was sweeping into action, particularly in countries which had never before seen a Mini, and particularly in North America. BMW had always considered that they would like to sell the MINI in the United States, sometimes there were doubts about its viability because the old Classic Mini had been a forgotten car for many years (no Minis had been sold to the USA after the 1960s, nor to Canada after the late 1970s). Only enthusiasts, or European car fanatics, still knew what Mini-motoring was all about.

Even so, there were times when the marketing aspirations of the importers, and the realities of the engineers, did not match: 'At first,' Chris Lee says, 'the Americans were looking for supercar performance, with 0–60mph times in around six seconds!'

The launch in North America was scheduled for the spring of 2002, as the big buying season got underway, and the MINI was to be sold as a speciality product, not as a first car. Before that date approached,

Before I drove a MINI Cooper, BMW promised me a 'go kart' feeling. I got it – it was almost impossible to get the little hatchback to roll on tight corners …
(David Wigmore)

As if you needed to be reminded! The 'MINI' badge is discreetly displayed in the centre of each wheel. (David Wigmore)

Other testers don't like these silly door-closing bars, and neither do I. What is the betting against an early face lift? (David Wigmore)

Torsten Muller-Oetvoes was already clear: 'We will sell on the MINI's 'go-kart' driving feel, on its handling. It's the best fun-to-drive car in this price range. It's also a small car but a true premium car as well.

Incidentally, at 3.6 metres long, the MINI will be the smallest *real* car in the USA. That will be our Unique Selling Proposition.

'The older enthusiast customers are not who we will be looking for, but they are important for building up the reception for the new MINI, and as important contact persons. In the United States, the MINI will very often be the fourth or even the fifth car in a household. People who have a big interest in cars will buy this car because their idea of having more than one "fun car" in the garage is good. Not all of them will be existing BMW customers – some will, but there will be lots of new customers.'

Even before the end of 2001, though, BMW had started to ramp up its pre-launch activity for the new car. In mid-2001 a new MINI made its way over to Mini Owners Club meets in the USA, and there were other official sightings.

More ambitiously, the company took advice from its American advertising agents, and started what is trendily called 'guerilla marketing' – which really means gaining publicity by unorthodox means. All over the USA, and particularly in the big cities, BMW bought a fleet of big Chevrolet Suburbans, mounted a MINI on to the roof, and had the driver cruising the streets, all day and every day.

Knowing that many Americans liked to carry 'toys' like surfboards and jet-skis on the roof, the slogan on the side of the Suburbans was pure genius: 'Put the Fun Stuff on the Roof'.

Even before the MINI was officially launched, one BMW personality spent time driving a pre-production car around the streets of San Francisco, and was astonished by the interest, the sympathy and the sheer knowledge shown by bystanders: 'Whenever, wherever, we parked the car, there was tremendous interest. And why? I think because it is a car with a smiling face …'

Would this work well? Apparently it did, for on the 'Did you see …?' principle, the word got around even more quickly than expected.

USA sales of MINI Coopers, while vital to the viability of the programme, would naturally have to fit in with deliveries to all other markets. UK sales began in July 2001, building up slowly and steadily, then cars were released to Europe, and Japan was next on the priority list.

And, on Dr Diess's manufacturing list, this couldn't come soon enough: 'Once we have launched in Japan and the USA, we can then begin to think about the Cooper S, we can then start thinking about other engine derivatives, the diesel and more. Then there must be discussion about new derivatives of the car itself, and then about putting in a whole variety of customer option specifications.'

The point was clearly made that BMW was used to introducing new features on its more expensive cars, at first as optional equipment, then as specifications (and customers' expectations rose) seeing these features gradually filtering down into the smaller and less exclusive cars in the range. Before 2001, that lower limit was the 3-Series, but now there was the MINI to consider. How many other cars of this size, for instance, offer satellite navigation as an option?

Even at this stage, it was clear that the MINI was to be marketed in far more countries than the Classic Mini had ever been seen. By the 1990s, old-type Minis were being sold in Europe, and in Japan, to the exclusion of all other territories. For the new car, BMW was being far more ambitious. BMWs were already being sold in more than 140 countries – really in every country where there was the wealth and the economic activity to support a programme – and there seemed no reason why the MINI should not join them.

This would not, of course, be possible with Oxford limited to building just 110,000 cars a year, for it would surely make no sense to send too many small quantities of cars to 'marginal' territories. BMW, though, was typically bullish about the new car's prospects, pointing out that a third shift was always a possibility and

BMW has encouraged its chosen dealers to set up separate showrooms to sell MINIS – complete with a new corporate design.

that, in any case, CKD (Completely Knocked Down) assembly might also be considered: 'If there is a positive business case from our dealers,' Muller-Oetvoes commented, 'or from our subsidiaries, we would consider it. But they will have to build up a clearly-dedicated MINI team, and

BMW's new corporate design for its MINI showrooms has absolutely no links with the BMW marque. Many accessories were already available when the new car went on sale.

All Mini Coopers are built with the contrasting roof colour – white or black, depending on the base hue. Looks great on this small hatchback.

a certain investment in every territory will be needed. And about CKD? Over the next year or more, when assembly has been ramped-up, we must consider this. Really, you can build up from kits, anywhere. This is usually done for tax reasons.'

When BMW launched the new Mini in the UK, where better to pose it than London's Carnaby Street, where many original Mini trends were set in the 1960s?

In a special publication which appeared in Germany when the Mini first went on sale, BMW's Chairman, Professor Dr Joachim Millberg, made an interesting point in his Introduction: 'With Mini the BMW Group wants to address new, young, customer segments. Customers for whom the youthful and emotional character of the brand has an especially strong appeal. The kind of people for whose individualistic and unbounded lifestyle the Mini brand has been sculpted.'

Press reaction

BMW, it would be fair to say, waited rather anxiously for what the motoring press would say, once they had got their hands on the first test cars. The Mini's shape, after all, had been seen in public nearly four years before a tester ever slipped behind the wheel. The launch had gone well, and the arguments presented for the strategy had certainly been persuasive but BMW, in general, had suffered mixed reactions following their decision to dump Rover at what (to the public at least) was such short notice.

One faction saw this action as the result of hurt pride, of not being able to carry

124

through a project for the first time in decades, and of a previously-arrogant concern being made to look second-rate. Another – and perhaps this was predominant – was to see BMW as learning, sadly years too late, what had already been well-known to BAe, British Leyland and other managements before them. BMW, at least, got great credit for electing to hang on to the Mini brand, to preserve it, to invest heavily in it and now, to launch a new model to bring it back to life.

But was the new MINI, as a working machine, up to the mark? Press reactions, in general, agreed about the headlines – that this was a great car to drive ('a hoot' is how one newspaper described it), a fast and well-equipped little car and a worthy successor to the dear old Mini which had just died off. All of them, on the other hand, agreed on one drawback – that, in spite of its much larger stance, it had a disappointingly small cabin, particularly in the rear seats, where most testers found that with the front seats rolled well back, that the leg room was almost non-existent.

In May 2001 Britain's *Autocar*

Just before the MINI went on sale in the UK, BMW drove a press car round the streets of London, where it created quite a stir. Here it is, in the West End, standing out from normal London traffic.

magazine was the first English-language outlet to publish a detailed test, and in view of their multiple leak and sneak-preview pieces over the years, their conclusions were studied carefully. The following extracts tell the story:

The company which John Cooper founded, the John Cooper Works, introduced its 132bhp version of the MINI Cooper at the end of 2001. Conversion of the cars was to be carried out at the premises in Sussex, UK.

MINI
in North
America

When the new MINI went on sale in North America in 2002, it re-introduced a famous name to that continent after a gap of more than 20 years. Original-type Minis were sold in the USA until 1967, and were continued in Canada until the end of the 1970s.

Twenty-first-century MINIS, for sure, were more suited to North American traffic conditions than the originals had ever been. Not only were they faster and more able to keep up with normal traffic flows, but they were also much more sturdily built …

Michael Cooper, son of John Cooper and chairman of the John Cooper Works, with the first example of the 132bhp converted MINI Coopers, which went on sale at the end of 2001.

'No new car has been more eagerly awaited in the UK than BMW's interpretation of that great British institution, the MINI.

Reworking one of the twentieth-century's seminal automotive designs falls only a little short of raising the *Titanic* in the all-time list of difficult tasks. But your first glimpse of the MINI in traffic tells you just about all you need to know. It has been well worth the wait since the 1997 Frankfurt Show, because the MINI is as good a piece of retrospective car sculpture as we've seen.

The steering rack is quick. BMW has used one of the most aggressive racks it tested during development, and deliberately kept the steering effort high – an indicator of the strong dynamic theme.

The new car differs most from the original in its packaging, which is nothing like as space-efficient, and is probably best described as a two-plus-two.

The MINI tips the scales at a distinctly portly 1,125kg [2,481lb]. That's a big inhibitor, one it never overcomes.

[In performance] A great lugger it is not. Thank over-tall gearing for that. Sure,

the Mini has enough performance to make it fun, but it's no GTI. That in itself shouldn't be a problem for prospective customers, but the absence of any real character or panache in the drive train might be more of an issue. Considering its BMW parentage, this is a disappointing engine ...'

That, though, was the only serious criticism, for the team loved the handling:

'It also steers crisply, and there's no trace of kickback through the rim over rough surfaces, and it rounds corners with flair and precision and, most important, it rides beautifully. Above all, the new MINI is a comfortable drive, one whose suspension is as soothing over a rutted road as the first Mini's was crude. The best bit is the chassis' ability to involve you in the action ...'

In summary, *Autocar* awarded four stars (out of five), and made this summary:

'It would be easy to be seduced by the MINI's many charms and award it five stars. After all, it's a great looker that also happens to have one of the best front-drive chassis we've come across. It's great to look at and sit in, but not even the ride and handling or the superb build quality are strong enough to offset the mediocre engine and disappointing packaging. That's a shame, because here's a car every enthusiast naturally wants to like.

Don't get us wrong, the new MINI is a desirable car that has, for the most part, been brilliantly executed. But until the Cooper S arrives, bearing, we hope, a more characterful rather than simply a more powerful engine, it will remain short of genius ...'

Most test drivers agree on the car's qualities and – yes, let us be honest – its failings. When Michael Scarlett, a technical analyst of many years, collected his thoughts earlier

in 2001, he complained that the '... new MINI is effectively a two-seater, with strictly occasional back seats, unlike its namesake, and is of course anything but Mini in size and weight ...'

Personally, I thought I should hold fire until I was ready to write the book, and was relieved to find that my own impressions were like those of the other professional views. In performance, handling, steering and character, this was certainly the Mini of old – but this was demonstrably a more up-market motor car than the Classic Mini had ever been.

The cabin packaging – and both Rover and BMW will probably hate me for stating this – was severely compromised by the decision to fit a BMW 3-Series driving position into a larger-than-Mini cabin. I am a relatively tall man and when driving the MINI, if I was to be comfortable in the driving seat, there was little leg room for rear seat passengers: if space was made for them, it was well-nigh impossible for *anyone* to drive the car.

Yet the car sold well, from the very start, and continues to do so. OK, I give in – but I still think that BMW is selling a sporty-feeling 2+2-seater in the guise of a practical 'premium' small hatchback ...

The new, private-enterprise, John Cooper Works Club Sport MINI Cooper, fully race-prepared (including roll cage and all other safety equipment) was available for 2002 from Michael Cooper's operation in Sussex, priced at £16,420 (plus VAT, in the UK). The first scheduled appearance of such cars was at the Australian F1 GP, in Melbourne, in March 2002.

⊗ Cooper S
and Cooper S
'Works'
The high performers

By November 2001, therefore, the new MINI was already well established, though there was still much to do to flesh out the range completely. Production at Oxford was ramping up towards the plant's original capacity, a third shift was being planned, and BMW personalities were already talking warily about the derivatives which might follow by the mid-2000s. Although only 42,395 MINIs were produced in 2001, a year later that annual output would rocket to 160,037.

Late in 2001, BMW's hard-working staff reaped great publicity by their ability to attract part-time contract labour in Oxford, for a decision to introduce a three-day 'weekend shift' attracted students and housewives, who rapidly came to terms with 11 hour shifts when they realised that the reward was then £12.52 an hour. This addition pushed up the workforce to about 3,500, and the plant was positively buzzing. That workforce would expand even further in the years which followed.

BMW was already talking about increasing plant capacity to 180,000 cars a year, though little more could then be done without further, major, investment in an already crowded complex. That investment – both in plant and personnel – would not be long delayed, for by 2004 annual

production had reached more than 175,000 – as near to flat out as could be expected. The project which had looked a little like a gamble in the late 1990s was already turning into a money-spinner.

Right from the start, BMW had made it clear that the MINI was to be a separate brand, not merely another BMW model, and that it would evolve completely separately from any other car which BMW would produce. This meant that sub-derivatives and variants could all be spawned from the new front-wheel-drive base. This strategy was confirmed before the end of the year, when BMW stated that it was also developing yet another generation of front-engined/rear-driven cars, these being the new generation 1-Series BMW models which went into production at Regensburg, in Germany, in 2004.

By the end of 2001, too, BMW appeared to have made its peace (in public, at least) with Rover, and the Gaydon design/engineering centre in particular. In a very genial ceremony held on the floor of the BMIHT museum at Gaydon in October, BMW Board member Dr Werner Saemann handed over a new MINI for permanent exhibition among a range of old-type Classic Minis.

S for Sporting on the MINI Cooper S.

This compact CVT (Continuously Variable Transmission) automatic gearbox figured in the MINI options list from 2002. In Steptronic mode, there were six fixed forward ratios.

BMW previewed the MINI Cooper S in October 2001, stating that it would go on sale in 2002. Visually, the only change in front-end style was the addition of a cool air scoop in the bonnet pressing, to channel air towards the engine intercooler.

At the presentation, the line-up of cars – the new-generation silver-and-black MINI Cooper was flanked by the original 'Old Number One' 1959 Morris Mini Minor (the pilot-build car which had been the first down the assembly lines at Cowley), and Paddy Hopkirk's legendary 1964 Monte Carlo Rally-winning Mini Cooper S – emphasised just how much larger and more up-market the new model had become. It also emphasised how far MINI design had advanced in four decades. Most important, though, this display, side-by-side,

demonstrated how one type simply could never be confused with the other.

In handing over the car to Bob Dover (who was chairman of the BMIHT Board of Trustees), Professor Saemann made one very perceptive comment: 'The Mini is probably the best-loved car in the world,' he said, 'and the new MINI maintains the tradition of the classic 1960s icon, by spreading smiles wherever it goes. The Heritage Centre has by far the most exciting and valuable collection of Minis in the world, so it is fitting that this new family member should find a home here.'

Dr Saemann had homed in on a very obvious point – that the Mini *and* the MINI were both cars which made onlookers turn in the street, gaze lovingly, and grin. Both were that sort of car.

Bob Dover was equally enthusiastic, and made sure that the new car's heritage was made clear: 'It is easy to see that the new MINI is a worthy successor in concept and execution to Alec Issigonis's original vision ...'

Both mentioned the fact that the new MINI had been built at Oxford, which was also the plant where 'Old Number One' and the 1964 Monte-winning car had been constructed.

Even at this stage, only months after the new car had gone on sale, it was already clear that the MINI family was destined to expand steadily in future years, like other cars from the BMW stable (the 3-Series being a perfect example). In addition to the original hatchback, it was thought that in the future the MINI family might also include an estate car, a convertible, a coupé or even – dream on, enthusiasts – a two-seater sports car.

However, this process was always going to take time, and no visually-different MINI derivatives were thought likely to appear in public until 2003 at least. Those derivatives, whatever they were, would undoubtedly be assembled at Oxford. Modern car plants have such sophisticated assembly equipment ('fixtures and fittings' is how an estate agent might describe

them) that without a massive duplication of tooling it was difficult to see how a MINI derivative could be assembled in any other BMW plant, even if there was space to do so.

At the time, BMW-Oxford's Plant Director, Dr Herbert Diess, told me that when the factory's facilities were being revamped in 2000–2001, the strategy was always to make Oxford an ideal plant for producing only one type of car – one type, please note, not just a single model of that type: 'We couldn't make any other types here, they will have to be based on the MINI. Paint shops are usually flexible, and assembly lines are normally quite flexible. The complicated area, as you will understand, is the body-in-white area. But we have laid down the plant to build different derivatives of the same car. Some preparation work has been done, and we would need different body framing areas to deal with different shapes, but the areas and the planning are already there.'

By 2004, after the Cabriolet had been launched, it was clear that even this differently-constructed car had involved much extra work inside the factory buildings, which had been extensively modified only a few years earlier. By that time the modernised factory was almost full: no space was being wasted.

Widening the range

Even before the MINI Cooper S derivative was previewed in October 2001 (by that time BMW had stopped denying that such a model was on the way), the company had already mapped out its new-model launch strategy for future years. In 2001, Torsten Muller-Oetvoes commented: 'In marketing terms, I am already thinking up to five years ahead, and in strategic planning terms ever further ahead than that. We already know, we have already decided, what new MINI derivatives will be announced in a year, and in two years. Even new trim and colour schemes need to

On the MINI Cooper S, which went on sale in 2002, the new model was instantly recognisable at the rear with its top tailgate spoiler, its twin centrally-mounted exhaust tail pipes, the extra air vents in the lower bumper, and of course the unique badge on the hatchback lid.

The MINI Cooper S of 2002 had a 163bhp supercharged version of the Chrysler-designed 'Pentagon' engine, a new six-speed Getrag transmission, along with 195/55-16 tyres on a new wheel style, and the rear roof spoiler. Its top speed was likely to be at least 135mph.

be planned up to two or more years ahead.'

Speculation, even informed speculation, was bound to surround an important new range like this one. Even BMW, who look upon business as something to be carried out soberly, efficiently, and without frivolity, dropped a few broad hints as to how they might add to the MINI's appeal in the future. In particular, they used the official launch, at the Paris Motor Show of October 2000, to float a few computer-generated ideas of what differently-shaped models might look like. Some, but by no means all, of those developments reached the market place by the mid-2000s: others were either abandoned, or remained under wraps.

Automatic transmission

Early in the life of the MINI, BMW revealed that it would soon be offering some MINI One and Cooper models with a CVT (Continuously Variable Transmission) type of automatic transmission. This derivative, in fact, finally reached the showrooms early in 2002 as optional equipment.

But would an automatic transmission option be popular in all markets? On the

old-type Mini, which had much less power, a British AP four-speed automatic had been optional on some models for many years, but it sapped the already limited performance, and was always treated as a rather expensive but endearing gimmick. In the new MINI, where there was much more power available, it was always a viable option, even when linked to the lowest-powered petrol-engined (90bhp) MINI One. The problem, in fact, was not going to be one of performance, but of price. In 2002, the automatic transmission cost £980 – an on-cost which was perhaps acceptable in the MINI-Cooper; but in a One which cost only £10,300?

BMW marketing staff, though, were quite convinced: 'Automatic transmission is very important,' Torsten Muller-Oetvoes insisted before the option was launched, 'especially when you look at the United States market. The MINI needs automatic transmission, and it will get a CVT type.'

Although CVT transmissions have been around for many years (DAF, after all, produced cars in the 1960s with infinitely-variable belt-drive layouts), they did not gain true acceptance until the 1990s, when

In October 2001, BMW handed over a new MINI Cooper to the British Motor Industry Heritage Trust, for display at Gaydon. Here Dr Werner Saemann discusses the project, while the Chairman of the BMIHT Trustees, Bob Dover, listens.

The car was most aptly flanked by 'Old Number One' (621 AOK, the original 1959 Mini) and by Paddy Hopkirk's 1964 Monte Carlo Rally winning car. The last Classic Mini of all is in the glass case which can be seen behind Dr Saemann's head.

This cutaway image of the MINI Cooper S shows just how full of kit this compact little front-wheel-drive machine actually is.

large concerns like Ford-Europe and Fiat embraced the technology. By using a complicated internal system of drive belts and variable diameter drive pulleys, sophisticated electronic controls could sense (and balance) road speed and torque demands, while keeping engine revs virtually constant. To anyone unfamiliar with such a transmission, the constant-speed sound emitted was eerie – but if that was ignored, the effect was fascinating.

MG, which was still controlled by BMW when development began, had offered a 'Stepspeed' version of a CVT automatic transmission in the MGF sports car from 1999, which gave the company much early experience (though on a limited-production scale) of this new ZF-derived layout.

In the MGF, the ZFST CVT system coped admirably with 118bhp from the Rover K-Series engine, so a developed version (much improved with input from consulting engineers, Ricardo) would have no trouble in dealing with the power of the MINI One and Cooper models, though in the long term it was not to be available (or, it seems, demanded) in the Cooper S.

Nor did an owner merely have to slot the gearlever into D-for-Drive and let the electronics do the rest, for there was also provision for a semi-automatic, change-fixed-ratios-oneself, operation. What BMW always knew as a 'Steptronic' change – which was excellent, and had a real sporty feel (as I know so well, from my long experience of owning larger BMWs) – became part of the MINI package, when six

fixed ratios, instead of the continuously-variable mode, were available.

Cooper S – a legend reborn

It took time – until October 2001 – but, as forecast so many times over the years when the new model was being developed, BMW finally unveiled the third major derivative of their new car, the supercharged MINI Cooper S. Since the new MINI was then being launched, in Japan, at the Tokyo Motor Show (Japan was a country where the classic Mini-Cooper had always sold well), the company were absolutely right to show off a new model to a territory which seemed sure to buy tens of thousands in future years.

Even more than 'MINI Cooper', this was the new brand name which enthusiasts had been waiting for. Way back in the 1960s, it was the Cooper S which had generated so many of its own legends. Not only had Paddy Hopkirk won the Monte Carlo rally, but so had Timo Makinen, while Rauno Aaltonen had not only won the RAC rally in 1965, but the European Rally Championship in the same year. Then, of course, there were the 'works' supported racing cars, which won events all round Europe. When rallycross was invented, the nimble little front-wheel-drive Cooper Ss soon proved to be ideal for that sport too.

As a production car, the classic Mini Cooper S had always sold well. Although Lord Stokes's British Leyland had killed it off in 1971 (British Leyland did not, it seemed, want to go on paying royalties to John Cooper for the use of his name. How short-sighted can you get?), it had to be revived, by popular demand, for the 1990s. As the Mini Cooper S brand had always been a profitable derivative, a relaunch under BMW ownership was almost inevitable. This time around, though, the Cooper S would not have a super-tuned normally aspirated power unit, but would have forced induction. For the very first time on a Mini-badged car, a supercharger (not a turbocharger), would be standard equipment.

Before it arrived there was much speculation about the specification of the new car, and sneak illustrations were published in the more excitable motoring magazines for months beforehand. When the official preview came, therefore, the public knew almost exactly what to expect.

BMW, with the help of consulting engineers Ricardo, was proud of what had been achieved. Rover, in fact, had already been working hard on the new Mini Cooper S at Gaydon, but the project was by no means signed off when the entire Mini development programme was thrown into disarray as the BMW-Rover 'divorce' erupted in the spring of 2000.

Still under BMW management and control, work on the new model was swiftly transferred to Ricardo's Midlands Technical Centre at Leamington Spa (just a few miles away) and brought in, on time, in a remarkable joint effort. BMW was grateful – and gracious – about this achievement: 'Ricardo got involved at a critical stage', Mini product manager Sven Wood later confirmed.

Although the exterior style seemed to be little changed – at a casual glance (but look further!) the only obvious tweaks were to provide a forward-facing air inlet/scoop in the bonnet, and twin exhaust pipe outlets under the centre of the rear bumper – there was much more. Not only were the bumpers subtly more prominent, but there were new, mesh-covered, vents at either side of the exhaust outlets, while the wheel-arches were subtly flared, and a rear roof spoiler was also standard.

In addition, there was much innovation crammed in under the skin. First of all, the Cooper S's engine power output had been pushed up to a rousing 163bhp at 6,000rpm, which seemed sure to turn this into a 135mph car. That figure had been achieved with the help of a small, high-revving, supercharger (not a turbocharger – for BMW apparently wanted to use the supercharger's great merit of boosting from really low revs, and being instantly 'on call' when the throttle was opened).

This was the very first time that BMW (or, for that matter Rover, though they were never part of the engine tuning decision-making process) had used a positively-driven supercharger installation. Previous Mini-based cars like the Metro Turbo had used a turbocharger instead.

To keep everything within bounds, the nominal compression ratio had been dropped from 10.6:1 (normally aspirated Mini Cooper) to 8.3:1 (Mini Cooper S), the new engine also having different pistons, valves, and a modified electronic engine management system. Cool air was channelled direct to the supercharger, which compressed it to provide up to 0.8 Bar/11.5 psi of extra pressure. The boosted air was then fed through an air/air intercooler, which was a bulky affair which had somehow been squeezed into the already full engine bay, by placing it on top of the engine itself. The bonnet scoop, in fact, channelled a blast of cooling air direct to the intercooler from the outside world.

This power figure (which was 48bhp above that of the Mini Cooper) had been so

The supercharged Mini Cooper S engine is very neatly packaged, with the air-to-air intercooler mounted on top of the camshaft cover, linked to the mechanically-driven supercharger by an alloy casting.

135

widely trailed in previous months that it was almost passed over. Indeed, it was the fitment of an all-new six-speed, all-indirect Getrag manual transmission which was of higher technical interest. As already detailed in earlier chapters, Rover had fought hard to retain its own-brand of Rover R65 gearbox on the original cars, but then had to admit that this simply could not cope with the increased torque (155lb ft/210Nm) of the Cooper S engine.

To solve their problem, BMW therefore turned to one of their most favoured suppliers, Getrag, which was already providing hundreds of thousands of transmissions every year for other, and larger, BMWs. Getrag, who had originally hoped to get the contract for providing the entry-level transmissions too (they would finally get their wish in 2003/2004), took a deep breath, and evolved their own-brand of three-shaft six-speeder which (though they never spelt it out at the time) would surely be able to cope with the 200bhp Alpina and John Cooper 'Works' derivatives which were forecast to follow.

Other chassis features matched the more powerful engine and the new gearbox – sports suspension, bigger wheels and tyres (195/55-16 run-flat tyres were standard,

and 205/45-17 tyres were optional), Automatic Stability Control (the opposite of ABS, as far as wheelspin is concerned), Traction Control, six airbags instead of four, a new central exhaust outlet position, and a retouched interior. Inside the car there was a brushed aluminium effect dash panel, and sports front seats were standard, along with leather trim for the steering wheel and gear lever.

All this, though, was rather premature information, for BMW was not ready to set prices until January 2002, and the first deliveries were not made until June of that year. In January 2002, when the MINI Cooper cost £11,600, BMW set the price of the MINI Cooper S at £14,500. Although this represented a £2,900 increase over the Cooper, it was still totally competitive with its rivals, and demand took off like a rocket.

Clearly this was a package that appealed to thousands of front-wheel-drive enthusiasts, and for a time a waiting list built up, especially in North America where the MINI had just gone on sale. Not only had an icon been reborn, but specification levels were very high, and with the ability to spring to 60mph from rest in no more than seven seconds this was the sort of 'pocket rocket' which had always been expected.

Press reaction

When the motoring press got its hands on the MINI Cooper S, they were ecstatic. The original MINI Cooper, they had suggested, did not have an engine worthy of its chassis – but the forced-induction Cooper S was different.

Britain's most authoritative motoring weekly, *Autocar*, thought that it was 'Not the fastest hot hatch, just the most entertaining'; that it was 'Funky, interesting and brilliantly styled'; and that it was 'The most fun you'll have with front-wheel-drive': 'The S is all about usable everyday performance. Its power and torque characteristics have so clearly been shaped to satisfy those demands that you could argue the figures it posted in our

MINI Cooper S types have twin exhaust outlets under the centre of a restyled rear bumper.

MINI in North America

When the new MINI went on sale in North America in 2002, it re-introduced a famous name to that continent after a gap of more than 20 years. Original-type Minis were sold in the USA until 1967, and were continued in Canada until the end of the 1970s.

Twenty-first-century MINIs, for sure, were more suited to North American traffic conditions than the originals had ever been. Not only were they faster and more able to keep up with normal traffic flows, but they were also much more sturdily built …

Once launched, sales increased rapidly. 24,590 MINIs were sold in the USA in 2002, and another 36,010 followed in 2003. Part of the favourable publicity, and the rapid build-up of image, came by word of mouth, but some undoubtedly came from the way the cars starred so spectacularly in the remake of the film *The Italian Job.*

By that time the USA had become the MINI's second-largest sales market. No wonder, therefore, that the MINI was voted North American Car of the Year in 2003. In August 2004, too, it was fitting that the 500,000th new MINI was earmarked to a North American customer, who was flown in to collect his new car.

The MINI Cooper was voted North American Car of the Year in 2003, so BMW celebrated the award in the most extrovert manner.

hands are irrelevant … There's usable shove from as low as 2,500rpm and it doesn't begin to tail off until the far side of 6,000rpm.

'Sound effects from the supercharger are reserved for full-throttle acceleration, but coupled with an authentically naughty exhaust note, the S makes all the correct noises …' All in all, the Cooper S was summarised as 'The Most Complete Hot Hatch Ever', and 'Few cars are blessed with as competent a basic platform, and with a sizeable chunk of BMW magic to finish it off, the rest was inevitable. Just how completely it adds up on the road and as an everyday experience is a genuine shock though: fast, nimble and terrific fun on the move, and with an even bigger helping of style, thanks to the cosmetic tweaks … the cute styling, solid image and excellent residual values will obliterate all else. Pile in that fun factor and you're left with the definitive small fast car.'

All this, incidentally, went with facts and figures confirming a 133mph top speed (in fifth, rather than sixth, gear, which was really an overdrive), 0–60mph in 7.6 seconds, and overall fuel economy which could still approach 30mpg (Imperial) if the driver could restrain himself.

No one, but no one, ever seems to drive a MINI Cooper slowly, because the supercharger response is instantaneous.

Yet this was only the start, for before long it became clear that BMW was determined to hang on to the Mini heritage with the new MINI Cooper S, but to boost it for all it was worth. Not only was the John Cooper connection preserved (after the founder had died, his son Michael vigorously kept up the good work), but 1960s Mini legend Paddy Hopkirk was hired to use all his well-known Irish presentation skills, and to be seen with the MINI on many important occasions.

The personal touch

Even before the MINI Cooper S was previewed, the John Cooper Works, whose founder John Cooper had been taken into BMW's confidence at a very early stage, had already prepared its first performance conversions. Led by John's son, Michael, who had become Chairman of the operation, the Sussex-based team revealed the John Cooper Works engine conversion of the MINI Cooper (not the Cooper S – though that would follow) at the end of November 2001.

The result of an 18-month development programme, this saw peak power boosted from 115bhp to 132bhp, which was achieved by providing a replacement cylinder head. This not only ran at a compression ratio of 10.9:1, but the ports had been gas-flowed, matched, and polished, and there was a free-flow air filter system and an all-new rear stainless steel exhaust system. For a price of £1,750 (plus, in the UK, VAT and fitting charges), this conversion included rebuilding of the engine in the Cooper workshops at East Preston, near Worthing, plus the distinctive addition of special 'Works' badging and other cosmetic details.

As Michael Cooper stated: 'My father was very proud that BMW chose to apply the Cooper name to the performance versions of the new MINI … His involvement with BMW's development of the new MINI from the beginning of the project also fuelled his interest in producing engine conversion kits for the new car.

Following his death late last year, I was equally determined to introduce the "Works".'

200bhp and front-wheel-drive

Early in 2003, Michael Cooper's ultimate weapon, the MINI Cooper S 'Works', was ready for sale. Like the MINI Cooper 'Works' conversion, this was to be available either as an aftermarket installation installed at the John Cooper Works in Sussex, or as a retrofit kit. For all MINI enthusiasts, though, the great news was that it had been completed with the full backing of BMW. Not only did the manufacturers' warranty stay intact, but the kits could be fitted at any official MINI dealership from April 2003.

The Cooper S 'Works' conversion had been brewing for many months, for both Michael Cooper and BMW wanted it to be as near a production-line car as possible. They were not, it seems, likely to approve any other type of conversion: 'Because we make the only "official" car,' Cooper insisted, 'there's no question of us going outside the rules. Creating a car with the reliability to deserve a full BMW warranty meant it had to be tested to destruction. But we're pretty delighted with what we've come up with. And so, I believe, is BMW.'

Although all the basic ground work was carried out in West Sussex, BMW was always looking over Cooper's shoulder, and the result was one of which they approved, one which met all their standards. To Cooper, more used to a more relaxed attitude to perfection, this was strange, but to a company like Alpina (who apparently could not produce the same sort of transformation at a sensible price) it would have been normal.

Noisy exhaust note? Certainly not. A rock hard ride? Not likely. Extrovert 'Lads Mags' looks and character? No way.

The 'Works' conversion centred almost totally on the engine, though it was also possible to specify 18in wheels to add to the package. 18in wheels? Good grief –

some of us remember when Mini wheel sizes went up from 10in to 12in in the 1970s, and thought the end of the world had come …

In gaining an extra 37bhp over the standard car, the secret was not in screwing up the installation to insane boost levels, but in replacing the supercharger completely, though without disturbing the original (and rather complex air-flow pattern) of the standard car. Bolted, just as before, to the cylinder block, and facing forward towards the front grille, the 'Works' supercharger was larger, and better

Michael Cooper outside John Cooper Garages, where all the 'Works' conversions are carried out.

able to cope with increased airflow.

The cylinder head was reworked, part of the exhaust system was opened up (but the catalytic converter remained in place so that all exhaust emission regulations were satisfied), and the peak boost was increased.

It was the boost increase – from 0.7Bar to a full 1.0 Bar – and the fact that the engine peaked at 6,950rpm instead of 6,000rpm, which helped push up peak power to a rousing 200bhp. More than that, peak torque leapt from 155lb ft (standard S) to 177lb ft, making the S 'Works' feel altogether more lusty and broad-shouldered than ever before.

With all that torque available, those sensationally-styled 18in wheels almost became a 'must', for with more rubber actually on the ground they were better able to deal with the extra power.

The performance was – well, 'sensational' comes to mind. With a top speed approaching 140mph, 0–60mph was available in no more than 6.8 seconds (wheel-spin being a problem!), while 0–100mph came up in 17.2 seconds.

But it wasn't the performance figures alone which made this car so appealing. It was the sort of machine that not only looked aggressively fast, but steered, stopped, and handled in the most emphatic

Love that registration number! Michael Cooper's 'Works' demonstrator outside John Cooper Garages' Sussex premises.

in-your-face manner. Some cars inspire respect, some fear, and some boredom – but in the case of the S 'Works' the effect was usually to inspire excitement, enjoyment, and pure, unadulterated, fun. To quote *Autocar* magazine: 'The S Works is not a car you're going to buy because it represents terrific value. It's a much more emotional, and far less rational, product than that. You will buy this car because you'll take one look at it and fall hopelessly in love ...'

Depending on the labour charges levied by an individual dealership when converting the standard car, the transformation to 'Works' specification cost over £3,000. At an April 2003 launch price of £18,074 ('on the road') for a fully converted and warrantied MINI Cooper S 'Works', this was the most expensive new MINI so far launched. That was before the many extras available on such cars could be added up. Everything from the 'Salt', 'Pepper', and 'Chili' packs, to leather upholstery, automatic air conditioning, and a satellite navigation system, could keep the invoice growing. It was not difficult to pay more than £25,000 for such a car.

This did not seem to deter buyers, especially in territories like the UK, USA, and Germany, where the new MINI had become, and remained, one of the most trendy, desirable and – yes – downright cute new cars on the market.

The 'MINI Cooper S Works' was so successful that within 18 months well over 6,000 such kits had been sold: 36 per cent of these went to customers in the USA and 21 per cent to British customers, the next most important markets being Germany, Italy, and Japan. For 2005, in any case, the 'Works S' engine was to be tuned even further – to 210bhp, with 179lb ft of peak torque – and the number of retro-fit options was to be increased, by offering an engine compartment suspension cross-brace and a new carbon-fibre rear spoiler.

As with the old-type Mini-Cooper S, it seemed, there was much that could be done, and new kit was being developed all the time.

Already a success?

Even so, cuteness is one thing, but commercial success is quite another. Back in Munich, BMW's accountants needed to

With a MINI Cooper S 'Works', the logo on the front wings tells its own story.

The
Italian
Job

Because the original Mini had starred in the original *Italian Job* movie of 1969, it was almost inevitable that a remake would follow in 2003. Although the title remained, vast amounts of money were involved, and three new-generation Minis shared an integral role in the movie, there was otherwise no connection between the plots of the two films.

Naturally the climax of the new film featured a fast and furious car chase. This time round, however, the action took place in, and under, Hollywood Boulevard in Los Angeles in the USA. Two Mini Coopers and one Mini Cooper S, laden with gold bars, provided all the action, but during the course of the filming BMW Group provided Paramount with no fewer than 32 Minis. In the film, need it be said, UK origins were emphasised because the three Minis were decked out in (Chili) red, (Pepper) white, and (Indi) blue!

Released in the USA in May 2003, and in the UK in September, the new *Italian Job* movie was controversial. Diehards thought it should have stuck closer to the original storyline, but most action-seekers enjoyed the sight of Britain's trendiest new car showing off its agility and dauntless character.

Once the Mini hit the streets in the USA, a remake of The Italian Job *was almost inevitable. This time around, Hollywood-style, all the stunt driving was in Los Angeles, not only in the Subways ... but in the famous dried-up watercourse of that great city. As in the original film, the Minis got away with the loot!*

The John Cooper 'Works' model was further improved for 2005. These smart 18in road wheels are one of the features.

know that their huge gamble – in retaining the MINI brand, in uprooting the Cowley/Oxford facilities, and in backing their gut feeling that *this* was what the motoring world needed – was going to pay off. £280 million, after all, had been invested at Oxford since 2000, and many thousands of workers – staff, agency employees, and suppliers' staff – relied on MINI for their livelihood. Not only that, but the original pricing had been set as low as possible, and profit margins were reputedly

not as high as on other mainstream BMW products.

Two years on from the day that deliveries began in 2001, the company began to feel more relaxed about the project. Oxford's facilities had been re-jigged, then re-jigged again, so that now it was possible to make up to 600 MINIs every day. The new MINI was already available in more than 70 territories, and it was good to know that 75 per cent of the output was being exported.

To BMW's relief and great satisfaction, the new MINI sold best of all in the UK (where its heritage lay), in the USA, and in Germany. Getting back into the British market was important, for the old Mini had been left to dribble along, unloved and un-marketed, in the 1990s. 11,628 new MINIs had been sold at home in the first year, 35,545 in 2002, and it looked as if more than 40,000 would follow in 2003.

Part of this success was due to the quirky MINI character which emerged. In particular the 'MINI Adventure' series of snappy TV and cinema adverts made the new car instantly trendy, while the car's rock-solid build quality impressed North Americans in a way that the old Mini never had.

The miracle was that this early success had been achieved from a standing start, with only part of a complete range. The new MINI family would not be mature until a diesel-engined version and a convertible were added – and that was about to happen.

Stunt driver Russell Swift needed no further invitation. Once put anywhere near a MINI, he had it up on two wheels in a trice. Some transmission trickery was needed, so don't try this at home …

9 Diesel and Cabriolet

Building the family

In the meantime, BMW had been busily working on an extension to the MINI range – but in another direction. For 2003, instead of providing yet more MINI performance, they were looking for better fuel economy.

Like most of their rivals, BMW's way of doing this was to provide diesel power. Not, you understand, by developing a diesel-fuelled version of the 16-valve 'Pentagon' power unit, but with a different engine altogether.

The launch of a diesel-powered version of the MINI was inevitable – inevitable even at the project stage – for one simply couldn't launch a new 'people's car' these days without providing the option of a diesel engine. In some sales territories, where diesel fuel was much cheaper than petrol, and where the tax regime also favoured diesel, this could literally make or break a new car's prospects. Although MINI customers in the USA might not be interested (even though modern common-rail diesel engines can now be so torquey and powerful, the North American market for diesel-engined cars is still tiny, and is likely to remain so), in the rest of the world a diesel derivative was bound to sell like five-cent hamburgers.

At the end of the 1990s, however, BMW had a problem. Although their own diesel engines were technically advanced and successful, the smallest currently available was the 1.95-litre 'four'. This was being built at Steyr in Austria for use in the

3-Series range (and, eventually, in the 1-Series). Not only was this engine too powerful for what BMW had in mind for the MINI, but it was physically too large and too heavy. Because BMW's own financial analysis then showed that heavy investment in an all-new layout could not be justified unless such an engine could find a home in other BMWs (or even other makes of motor car), they had to take a Brave Pill. For the first time, ever, they went out shopping among the world's other auto-makers.

Although such behind-closed-doors deals are being explored all the time today, such a process was not easy for BMW's directors, engineers, and planners to accept. First of all it meant making discreet approaches to companies which might be rivals in some ways; often it would be necessary to offer 'contra' deals to keep the other party happy; and always it was necessary to reveal some of the forward plans which BMW would otherwise have like to keep under wraps.

BMW was already supplying engines to other companies – larger/more powerful diesels to Opel, for instance – and at one time it had even discussed supplying diesels to Jaguar for the new Jaguar S-Type and X-Type ranges; but this was quite a restricted business. Once they had eliminated rival car-makers who would not willingly talk to them, companies whose engineering was not thought up to BMW's own standards, and others whose diesel

The MINI Cooper S Convertible in action.

Toyota built the diesel engine, BMW re-packaged and re-engineered it, and it became a neat fit in the MINI's engine bay.

designs were already looking old-fashioned, the choice was surprisingly limited.

Having started by surveying Europe, in the end BMW had to look further afield – to Japan. It did not take long to eliminate Nissan (linked to Renault), Mazda (to Ford), and Mitsubishi and Isuzu (both linked to General Motors), and BMW soon homed in on Toyota. Not only was Toyota the largest Japanese car-making giant of all, with several already-established European links, but it is the world's third-largest car-maker and was totally independent of links with other car-making groups.

Toyota, it was already known, had started work on an all-new small diesel design in 1998. It was preparing to launch a new, state-of-the-art (which meant using high pressure common-rail fuel injection technology, an exquisite tiny turbocharger which rotated at up to 225,000rpm, and ultra-clean exhaust gas technology) 1.4-litre power unit, first for its own Yaris hatchback and later, presumably, for other models in Toyota's vast range. Because the Toyota Yaris was smaller, less powerful, and considerably cheaper than the forthcoming MINI, neither Toyota nor

BMW saw any clash of interests, and a deal looked promising.

This looked liked a marriage made in heaven, for BMW soon discovered that the new engine, which Toyota coded IND-TV, was going ahead to an ideal timetable. BMW could not use a small diesel before 2002 – and they discovered that the IND-TV was to go into mass production at precisely that time. Previewed at the Frankfurt Motor Show of September 2001 for the Yaris, Toyota announced that this engine was due to go into mass-production in the first half of 2002. Although originally there were stories that it was to be manufactured in Europe from 2003, this did not happen, and when BMW began to take supplies it was by sea, from a Toyota engine plant at Kamingo in Japan.

As previewed for the Yaris, the new unit was a neat and compact design, with the latest common-rail fuel injection technology. Even before BMW had approached Toyota, by the way, there was already a German connection, for Bosch provided the fuel injection technology.

The new engine had VVT (Variable Valve Timing), and was rated at 75bhp at

148

4,000rpm, with peak torque of 125lb ft at 2,000–2,800rpm. Incidentally, the quoted torque figure was higher than that developed by either of the One and Cooper's petrol-powered 'Pentagon' engines, which meant that the transmission would have a harder time.

In conjunction with BMW, who had an active part in the development process, Toyota pushed metal casting and stress technology to its limits. Not only was there an aluminium cylinder block *and* head, but the air-to-air intercooler also used an aluminium matrix. For packaging/installation reasons, the turbocharger housing was completely integrated into the exhaust manifold. Because of this attention to detail, the IND-TV weighed only 251lb/99kg. Although this was heavier than the 'Pentagon' petrol engine, it was commendably light for a diesel – all of which made it eminently suitable to power the new MINI.

It was too much to hope that such a new engine would drop straight into the MINI's engine bay, and be ideal. Nor was it. With Toyota's co-operation, Dr Petra's engineers contacted Bosch and eventually modified the power unit, with a higher-pressure Bosch fuel system (1,600 Bar instead of the 1,350 Bar chosen by Toyota), which boosted peak torque by a useful 7lb ft and made the car even more driveable.

There was a downside to this, however, because the diesel-engined MINI produced more peak torque than the One or Cooper derivatives. BMW therefore concluded that the original Rover R65 five-speed gearbox could no longer cope, and opted to fit a modified version of the Cooper S's six-speed Getrag box instead. Inevitably this resulted in a cost increase, but as it coincided with greater peace of mind this was accepted.

It wasn't long, too, before the team discovered that they would have to re-engineer the power-assisted steering (the existing electric motor and the engine were fighting for the same space), but this was speedily resolved by a different installation which carried a small penalty in operating fuel economy.

BMW could not originally credit the coincidence of the new engine's schedule, which was always working in its favour. When used in the Yaris, this new diesel engine would go on sale in Europe early in 2002. Customers (always the most severe 'development engineers' which any company could encounter) would be able to do their worst, in Toyota cars, and seek out any 'bugs' for more than a year before the MINI version was even available!

Light, compact, and undeniably right-sized for the MINI, this ultra-economical 75bhp unit was all set to make an ideal alternative buy for customers in countries like France and Italy, where diesel was rapidly becoming king. Because BMW was launching the MINI in more and more countries – more than 70 of them at this

BMW evolved its own version of Toyota's D-4D diesel engine for use in the MINI. Though UK sales were expected to be limited, countries like France and Italy accepted the MINI One D with open arms.

This was the only way that BMW identified the diesel-engined MINI – a discreet 'D' on the hatch.

The latest fascia, 2004 style, on the MINI diesel. Still as quirky as ever.

engined alternative on offer in the Classic Mini. As far as I know, because of the old car's unique engine-over-gearbox layout no ambitious private conversion was ever attempted. However, the Rover 100 (original titled the Mini Metro, of course), which died in the 1990s, had been offered with a 57bhp/1.5-litre normally-aspirated Peugeot diesel, best described as gutless and noisy into the bargain. No diesel engine fitted to the new MINI was ever likely to be like that.

When it first reached the European marketplace, early in 2002, in the Toyota Yaris, the new diesel engine was well-liked: its claimed fuel economy figures were quite remarkable. Even so, it was more than a year before the diesel-engined MINI was ready, and by this time the petrol-engined types had got something of a reputation for fuel-burning. Some sort of fuel-saving was needed, to make an impression.

BMW did not expect diesel-engined MINIs to make up the majority of production, but certainly needed their frugality in the southern European markets. According to original estimates, Toyota was only likely to supply up to 10,000 diesel engines a year, of which a mere 1,500 were expected to go to British customers. This was little more than five per cent of BMW-Oxford's annual output of MINIs – but others were sure that sales would rise as the new version's reputation became known.

The new diesel engine was only available as a variant of the MINI One, called the 'One D', with suitable badging on the lid of the hatchback. When originally put on sale in June 2003 its UK retail price was £11,390, compared with the £10,400 asked for the petrol-engined One. Customers therefore had to ask themselves if they were willing to trade much improved fuel economy against a ten per cent price premium, and many apparently decided to do just that.

It was rare, however, for a 'basic' One D to be built, for such cars came with steel wheels and without air-conditioning. Alloys cost just £270 more at launch, and air

time, a figure which was still rising – it needed such an option in a whole variety of markets. Modern diesel engines are remarkably powerful and fuel-efficient, and diesel prices tend to be much lower than petrol prices in some countries, which is a very important factor in today's motoring world.

Here, by the way, was a complete break from the MINI's past: in 41 years (1959–2000) there was never a diesel-

conditioning added just £600 to the showroom 'sticker' price. BMW's British MINI brand manager, Trevor Houghton-Berry, stated that it was rare to see any customer spend less than £2,000 to 'spec-up' their car.

Independent tests soon made the sort of noises which bring smiles to every salesman's face. *Autocar*, for instance, had this to say after driving a One D in 2003: 'Start up and the silence is overwhelming. Most oil-burners cough consumptively into life: this one breathes mountain air instantly. There aren't even any traces of vibration in the cabin … Below 1,000rpm there isn't much shove, but as it moves into its power band, the diesel has that smooth, creamy shove of power typical of a modern oil-burner'.

Like all modern turbocharged diesels, this engine felt best when working in the mid-range, and was a brisk little machine which could keep up with all other MINIs in traffic. It was the sort of range addition which looked set to fill up Oxford for a long time to come.

Time for refreshment

Although BMW rarely facelifts its cars – in other words, it tends not to make them look different – from time to time it brings forward a package of improvements. As far as the MINI was concerned, that time came in the summer of 2004. Just before the Convertible came on stream, a whole series of engine, transmission, and equipment updates arrived for all models.

The most significant changes were mechanical. To replace the Rover R65 gearbox which had been original equipment on One and Cooper models, BMW now specified a newly-developed five-speed Getrag. The last technical link with Rover, and Longbridge, was thereby severed.

On the Cooper S (and just in time to be used in all the Cooper S Convertibles), the supercharged engine was redeveloped, with peak power now up to 170bhp @ 6,000rpm: this meant that BMW now claimed a top speed of 138mph for the MINI Cooper S. Minor improvements had also been made to peak torque (but not peak power) in the MINI Cooper engine.

All in all, this was not a major carve-up. As Trevor Houghton-Berry said at the time : 'Clearly we did not want to change a winning formula … this model update is merely a few subtle tweaks to make the MINI even more desirable than it already is …'

BMW has always been anxious to stress the MINI's streetwise image. A diesel-engined car, ideal for London mews living? Of course!

Just in time for the launch of the Convertible in 2004, BMW refreshed the front-end style of all MINIS, notably by new-type headlamp clusters and removal of the original bumpers.

This is the Zenon headlamp cluster available on MINIS from 2004.

Opposite: By mid-2004, the Convertible style was available in One, Cooper, and Cooper S forms. At that time no diesel-engined variety was available.

Visually, there was little to see, though if one looked carefully there were new-type clear glass headlamps, redesigned front and rear bumpers, and repositioned reverse lamps. Inside the car, a raft of changes included more stowage space (and – important, this, for the Americans – a larger cup holder in the rear), extra fittings such as a side-mounted sun visor for the driver, and the standardisation of the rev-counter on the MINI One.

Not only that, but there were several new colours (which meant ten exterior colours for every MINI), and there were now 14 different cloth, cloth/leather, and leather interior trim packages.

To take account of all this, prices were increased by an average of 2.5 per cent, which meant that on-the-road MINI motoring now started at £10,780 for the One, and at £15,180 for the Cooper S; after which the customer could begin to load up the specification with extras. Hearsay suggests that it was easily possibly to up-spec a MINI Cooper S to well beyond £25,000, and that this had already been done several times …

At last, an open-top MINI

Convertibles – sometimes known as cabriolets, of course – are now back in a big way in Europe, so naturally the concept of a convertible MINI was floated at a very early stage. At first, though, there were mixed marketing signals for BMW to analyse. Way back in the 1980s and 1990s, old-type MINI convertibles had flopped – and the first factory-approved types did not appear until the original-style Mini had been around for more than 30 years. These were produced as well-equipped conversions by independent coachbuilders and were at once heavy, sluggish, and expensive.

BMW, on the other hand, could not ignore the successful sales garnered by companies like VW (with the Golf) and Peugeot (with the 206CC), nor the fact that arch-rival Mercedes-Benz had not yet attempted to put a drop-top A-Class on the market.

More than that, all the sales trends showed that new car buyers liked open-air motoring, even if this meant breathing in traffic fumes, and getting messy hair! In the UK alone, more than 100,000 new convertibles would be registered in 2004, and BMW's marketing experts reckoned that one in every five MINI sales could soon be of the Convertible variety.

Enthusiasts never dismissed the convertible concept from the future model. Even before the BMW-Rover divorce, we know that the company worked on such a car in 1999/2000 (designers even got down to the detail of how to install, operate, and furl the soft-top), but once the project finally returned to BMW, the convertible project had to wait its turn for resources. Like its rivals, such a car would need a

series of powerful engines to cope with the extra weight of a drop-top shell, but in the meantime, the thought of a Cooper S-engined MINI convertible was really mouth-watering.

BMW first admitted that a Convertible model was on the way in 2003, and the first official details were revealed in February 2004. Even so, the first Convertible deliveries were held back until July of that year, and the top-of-the-range MINI Cooper S Convertible followed in August. One, Cooper, and Cooper S types were all available, there being no apparent marketing demand for a diesel-powered version.

Although the running gear and basic 'chassis' of the Convertible was like that of the well-established hatchback, much work, innovation, and development expertise had gone into the revised body shell. The whole

This excellent cutaway shows the operation of the complex soft-top of the Mini Convertible.

of the rear of the shell had to be re-engineered, not only to provide a traditional Mini drop-down boot lid instead of the hatchback, but to make way for a cute pair of padded roll-over hoops behind the rear seats. Not only that, but BMW standards were applied to the folding and clamping mechanism of the electrically-operated top.

Drop top structures, by definition, are never as rigid as the hatchbacks from which they are derived, for the lack of a roof and rear quarter pillars means that the torsion box is always destroyed. Clawing back some of the rigidity is done by stiffening the understructure, but in the case of the Mini, BMW went one stage further. The invaluable 'ghosted' drawing on page 157 shows that much extra steel was therefore added to the sills under the doors, the rear quarter panels behind the doors, and the floor behind the seats. Not only that, but stout steel tubes were led up through the modified windscreen pillars – a feature which hid another story.

The frame of the soft-top itself was engineered with very sturdy supports, especially over the top of the door glasses. The front of the frame, when being erected, mated perfectly with the steel tube reinforcements in the top of the screen pillars. The entire electrically-powered furling/re-furling operation was carried out by pressing a button on the screen rail: sensors made sure that this could not be completely done while the car was actually in motion.

When opening up the hood, first of all the front fabric was folded back to what BMW christened the 'open sunroof' position: this could be achieved with the car in motion. Complete opening up was only then achieved by stopping, and pressing the button a second time. Apart from that, the driver did not have to be involved – no clipping, no covering up, nothing. The whole operation took a mere 15 seconds.

It wasn't until I saw the Convertible shell being built at Oxford that I realised just how different it was from the hatchback variety. Although both shells progress down the same highly-automated Body-In-White assembly line while being constructed, it needs all the most modern electronic programming and agility of the ranks of Kuka spot-welding robots to get it right every time.

BMW admitted that beefing up the Convertible's shell, and adding the bulky soft-top mechanism, meant that it was no less than 221lb/100kg heavier than the hatchback. On the road, I have to be honest, it certainly felt like it. With the soft-top erect, and with those clever hood side rails clamped into the windscreen pillar, the shell felt rigid enough: as expected, though, with the hood down, this was no longer the stiff roller skate we had come to expect.

Naturally, all this fresh air sophistication came at a price, there being a considerable premium over the hatchbacks. At a time, for instance, when Mini One hatchback prices started at £10,780, that of the equivalent Convertible was £13,325. It was only when I settled into the sports seats of a Cooper S Convertible with a typical number of extras that I realised I was about to drive a £20,000 Mini. I had *never*

experienced that Mini price level before. Too expensive? BMW didn't think so – and by all accounts the order book proved the point.

Not that this was the end. From 1 January 2005, BMW also made automatic transmission available on the Mini-Cooper S and Cooper S Convertible models, this being a new fixed-ratio six-speed system (not a CVT gearbox) which included a Steptronic mode, and Steptronic paddles behind the steering wheel. Priced at £1,050, this sounded very suitable for the Cooper S's power delivery, as did the further new option of a limited-slip differential.

And then?

By 2005, five years after the new-generation Mini had first appeared, there seemed to be little scope to expand the range of styles on offer. Even if there was, their launch would depend on many factors – available finance, available capacity at Oxford, and, of course, the marketing forecasts made for each type.

Off the record, some BMW personalities admitted that they had perhaps underestimated the worldwide demand for a new Mini, and that they had spent all

Left: When developing the Convertible, BMW retained all the passenger space, though the boot was necessarily smaller.

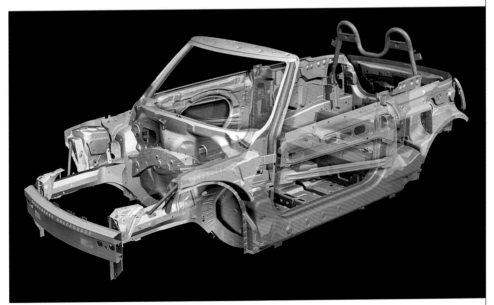

For the Convertible, the lack of a permanent roof meant a loss of stiffness. To provide more rigidity, BMW provided extra stiffening in the sills, in the rear floor, behind the doors, and with tubes up the screen pillars to link up with the sturdy soft-top frame when erect.

Fitting out the MINI Convertible with its soft-top on the assembly line at Oxford.

their time pushing out the limits at Oxford merely to satisfy orders for the hatchback and convertible derivatives.

Sometimes, though, BMW's grasp of MINI history was not perfect. By 2004, with annual MINI production at Oxford rising towards 200,000 units a year, it was suggested that this achievement was already higher than had ever been achieved by the 'classic' Mini. This might have been true of Mini assembly at Cowley/Oxford in the 1960s and 1970s, but not of Mini production overall. At its height, more than 300,000 old-style Minis were flooding out of Cowley/Oxford *and* Longbridge in a single year. Interestingly enough, the first 500,000 'classic' Minis had been produced in three years, so at that stage new and old were matching each other, figure for figure.

For all those reasons, the extra MINI derivatives which had been forecast in the motoring press *before* the MINI went on sale in 2001 no longer looked likely to appear. Not, at least, until a second-generation model takes over at Cowley, towards the end of the 2000s.

Perhaps, therefore, one could discount the following:

An estate car?

According to Rover design staff who 'talked out of school', in the late 1990s a MINI estate car ('Touring' in BMW-speak) was considered. The transverse-engined/front-wheel-drive layout of the production MINI would obviously be an ideal base. Way back in 1995, Rover marketing staffs reminded everyone in Munich that hundreds of thousands of old-style Classic Mini 'Countryman' cars had been sold.

Because the MINI car had a relatively low and squat cabin, and because its fore-and-aft styling lines were almost horizontal, it would be simple to 'grow' a three-door estate car/Traveller/Touring body style out of this, though it would be no great load carrier. With nostalgia in mind, it could also have been offered with decorative wooden members surrounding the window frames, wheel-arches, and rear loading door, and in North America it could then be called a 'Woody'.

The design studio at Gaydon had already worked up proposals for such a model in 1999. After project leadership reverted to Munich, Gert Hildebrand and Frank Stephenson of the BMW design team refined it further during 2000, yet by 2005 there had been no public sightings. Perhaps it would be delayed until the second generation MINI was launched.

A coupé?

Although this might sound mouth-watering for MINI high-performance enthusiasts, this was never going to be easy. As BMW's Munich design studio found in the mid-1990s, it was a most difficult style to graft on to the new MINI platform. One major problem (Alec Issigonis and his colleagues at the MG factory discovered this in the 1960s) would be to develop an attractive coupé style on a car with a lofty and immovable engine/transmission/suspension package up front, all hidden behind a relatively high, and bluff, front-end style. It was probably no coincidence that no such coupé project, or a related ultra-sporting two-seater, was

mentioned, even as a computer sketch, when MINI was officially previewed.

Options and Accessories

All the above, of course, would merely add to an existing 'cat's cradle' of options – 40 of them at first, double that number after the first few seasons – already available on MINI hatchbacks by 2005. Some were as functional as 17in road wheels (was £780 a bargain for the MINI-Cooper in 2001?), or automatic air conditioning (£830), while others were as frivolous as a leather-rimmed steering wheel (£80) or MINI-logo'd floor mats (£50).

More attractive, maybe, were the original three different options packages, which grouped together some of the individual items – 'Salt' adding interior trim items, 'Pepper' adding eight-spoke alloy wheels to the above, and 'Chili' factoring in a sports suspension package, 16in road wheels, and sports seats. 'Chili' added a rear roof spoiler too, which was not available individually.

Tens of thousands of option combinations were possible, and visitors to the Oxford plant would rarely seen two newly-built MINIs which were identical in every way.

The Alpina connection

Most intriguing of all was the thought of BMW's chosen high-performance associate, Alpina, being encouraged to develop white-hot versions of the Cooper or Cooper S types, this being a definite project in the early stages. In the 1980s and 1990s, after all, Alpina of Germany, under Burkhard Bovenseipen, had produced even-faster versions of almost every other BMW type, and could certainly wave a magic wand over any car that entered their workshops.

The chassis of the new MINI, of course, was already a fine and sorted installation, but still-larger wheels and tyres (hiding larger disc brakes) would make the little car's grip and security even more remarkable; while Getrag's brand new six-speed transmission, for sure, was engineered with higher power outputs in mind. Which only left Alpina to sort out the engine – but they had always been able to find more torque and higher revs in the past, so why not again?

Although the structure of the Convertible is noticeably less rigid than the hatchback, it remains a sturdy machine which handles well.

Sports
car
spin off?

By 2004/2005 some out-and-out enthusiasts were suggesting that BMW should develop a two-seater sports car based on the MINI's running gear. BMW listened politely, worked out the multi-million investment needed to produce a new product line, and kept their own counsel.

The obvious way to develop a MINI-based sports car, the enthusiasts thought, was to take what might be called the 'Toyota MR2' route. Moving the transversely-mounted MINI engine and transmission to a place behind a two-seater cabin would instantly produce a mid-engined car, whose suspension could be developed from existing MINI hardware. A completely new monocoque structure would be needed; in which case, enthusiasts asked, why not call the new car a Triumph …?

Such a car was engineered and partly developed, but late in 2002 news filtered out that the project had been cancelled. It was no coincidence, surely, that BMW had already put a lot of marketing muscle behind Michael Cooper's MINI Cooper S 'Works' project, which would have offered the same level of performance.

The Alpina-MINI, it seems, was also based on the MINI Cooper S, and had an enlarged, 1.8-litre, version of the supercharged 'Pentagon' 16-valve engine.

With more supercharger pressure, a freer-flowing exhaust system, and other tuning details, the engine was to be matched by larger wheels and tyres, and many other chassis tweaks.

The problem, it seems, was that costs eventually got out of hand. When news of the cancellation leaked out, an unidentified company insider was quoted as saying 'We could not have produced the car for a price the market would accept. There wouldn't be many customers for a £30,000 MINI.'

Just like old times! In the 1960s, anyone with a crazy idea usually applied it to a Mini. Now, the latest MINI comes in for similar style/taste attacks. Don't get too excited, though – BMW is not likely to put an ultra-long-wheelbase, six-wheeler MINI XXL on sale to the general public!

Onwards and upwards

By 2005, with the MINI well into its stride, BMW was cautiously proud of what had already been achieved. Demand was running at up to twice the rate originally predicted, and if the Oxford plant could only produce 200,000 MINIs every year it seemed certain that customers could be found for them. MINI was already being sold in more than 70 different markets, but (as company spokesmen gleefully reminded the motoring media) that left many other territories still unserved.

Although BMW was not about to reveal its next five-year plan, it had already confirmed two major innovations. First of all, there would indeed be a second-generation MINI (inspired guesses put the launch in 2007 or 2008), and it would be powered by a new-generation petrol engine.

Although the original BMW/Chrysler co-operation over the 'Pentagon' engine had worked quite well, development had had to be hustled through in the late 1990s, and the result had not come up to every

BMW expectation. The motoring press, used to smooth, high-revving power units from other car-makers, did not seem to be overly impressed and (of more importance to BMW) the fuel economy figures were not the best in class.

Because Chrysler had never taken up its originally-forecast 50 per cent share of output (the 'Pentagon' engine was made available in small Chryslers like the Neon, but never in the USA and only as an 'entry-level' power unit), while BMW had no other models in its big range where such power units could be used, the finances of the Brazilian plant, as it turned out, did not stack up in the way that they should have.

Because BMW was determined to make a success of the 'Pentagon' – technically, if not financially – it persevered with the 16-valve after Chrysler seemed to lose interest in it. For the future, however, it soon set out on the search for a replacement supply of engines. As with the diesel project (where it eventually made a deal with Toyota), the search for a new power unit was originally worldwide.

First you order your MINI, then you order the options. A sunroof (top left) or a Union Flag roof skin have both proved popular.

161

The MINI engine

Although the 'Pentagon' engine project (DaimlerChrysler say that they no longer recognise that nickname, by the way) was originally set up to benefit both MINI *and* Chrysler, in the end the American concern made little use of the engine which had largely been designed in Detroit.

To quote a DaimlerChrysler spokesman: 'There are three 4-cylinder engines built at Tritec: 1.4, 1.6, and 1.6 Supercharged. These engines are used (in varying assortment) in the MINI, the Chrysler Neon (outside North America), Chrysler PT Cruiser (outside North America), and the Chery A15 (which is a Chinese brand that mainly builds products for China).'

The vast majority of these engines were fitted to MINIs. After all, when did you last see a European-market Neon or PT Cruiser fitted with this power unit?

MINI assembly in full swing at Oxford. This is a Cooper S Convertible, with a sunroof-equipped hatchback close behind.

Before the end of 2004, in fact, it was an open secret that BMW was already developing a new, small, four-cylinder power unit in conjunction with the French PSA organisation (which was building Peugeots and Citroëns in very large quantities). This, they agreed, would one day supplant the existing petrol engine. But when? And would it come in advance of the next-generation MINI, or at the same time? At that stage, BMW was not saying – and no one could blame them.

In the meantime, much midnight oil was already being burnt in connection with new models, mainly back in Munich, though a small and specialised development team remained at Oxford. Perhaps there was no longer the sheer inventiveness of the late 1990s, when Wolfgang Reitzle's burning enthusiasm for new products inspired

everyone, but ambition remained.

For those who took the long view the new MINI story had, after all, only just begun, and all the pointers were upwards. No fewer than 176,000 MINIs had been delivered in 2003, even more were scheduled for 2004, and the 500,000th car eventually rolled out of Oxford in August, to be delivered to Dan Cowdry of California, USA.

In the beginning, when the completely rejuvenated plant had been equipped so speedily in 2000/2001, BMW had talked about producing only 100,000 MINIs a year. In the beginning there had only been a single working shift, but by 2005 the assembly lines were producing cars almost all the time. A three-shift system was being operated, seven days a week (there was a permanent weekend shift), and there was only a four-hour 'down time' spell every night for essential maintenance, cleaning and refurbishment to take place.

MINI production had started up in 2001 with 2,400 employees. By 2005 that had increased to 4,500, and growth seemed to be restricted more by the plant's physical limits than by demand. More than one in three of all newly-built MINIs were shipped overseas, first by rail from the company's own railhead (which linked up with the main Oxford-London line), then through a dedicated dock at Purfleet in Essex. This was a remarkable achievement.

In the meantime, the MINI was gradually shrugging off its final links with the old Rover Group businesses. Not only had BMW stopped taking Rover R65 gearboxes for One and Cooper types, but it had also set up alternative supply arrangements for some of the body pressings which had originally come from the Land Rover factory at Solihull. By 2004/2005, it seemed, more than half the content of a MINI was being supplied from European countries (and, of course, from Brazil), so this was by no means the British product that it might at first appear. When the second-generation MINI comes along, it seems that the process will be complete, and that here will be a European car which just happens to be assembled in the UK.

One final thought. More than five million of Alec Issigonis's original 'classic' Minis were eventually produced, though it took 27 years to pass that marker. Will the BMW-inspired MINI eventually beat all such records? And is anyone placing bets?

BMW celebrated building the 500,000th MINI at Oxford on 25 July 2004, little more than three years after the original deliveries had been made. The silver-with-black-striping MINI Cooper S was handed over to its North American customers the same day.

163

Specifications

Mini (introduced in 2001)

Layout
Unit-construction body/chassis structure, with steel panels. Three-door four-seat hatchback or Cabriolet, front-wheel-drive car.

Mini One

Engine

Type	BMW/Chrysler 'Pentagon' unit
Block material	Cast iron
Head material	Cast aluminium
Cylinders	4 in-line (transversely mounted)
Cooling	Water
Bore and stroke	77 x 85.8mm
Capacity	1,598cc
Main bearings	5
Valves	4 per cylinder, operated by single overhead camshaft and tappet fingers, driven by chain from crankshaft
Compression ratio	10.6:1
Fuel supply	Siemens EMS 2000 multi-point fuel injection, and engine management system
Max. power	90bhp (DIN) @ 5,500rpm
Max. torque	103lb ft @ 3,000rpm

Transmission (Manual)
Five-speed all-synchromesh manual gearbox: MG-Rover type to early 2004, Getrag thereafter

Clutch	Diaphragm spring, single plate

Overall transmission ratios

	MG-Rover	Getrag Type 252
Top	3.008	3.351
4th	3.748	3.921
3rd	4.740	5.231
2nd	6.924	7.954
1st	12.151	13.755
Reverse	12.730	13.434

Transmission (Automatic)
ZF, constantly-variable ratio (CVT) transmission

Overall transmission ratios

Forward gears	Constantly variable
Reverse	10.854

Suspension and steering

Front	Independent, coil springs, MacPherson struts, anti-roll bar, telescopic dampers
Rear	Independent, coil springs, multi-link location, telescopic dampers
Steering	Rack and pinion (power-assisted with electric and hydraulic assistance)
Tyres	175/65-15 radial-ply
Wheels	Bolt-on, steel
Rim width	5.0in on 15in wheels

Brakes

Type	Disc brakes at front, discs at rear, hydraulically operated, with anti-lock and servo-assistance as standard
Size	10.9in front discs, 10.2in rear discs

Dimensions
Track

Front	57.5in/1460mm
Rear	57.5in/1466mm
Wheelbase	97.1in/2467mm
Overall length	142.7in/3626mm
Overall width	75.8in/1925mm (across mirrors)
	66.5in/1688mm (across body shell)
Overall height	55.6in/1413mm
Turning circle	35ft 0in/10.7m (between kerbs)
Unladen weight	2,293lb/1040kg

MINI Cooper
As for Mini One, except:

Engine
Compression ratio	8.3:1
Max. power	115bhp (DIN) @ 6,000rpm
Max. torque	110lb ft @ 4,500rpm

Overall transmission ratios
	MG-Rover	Getrag Type 252
Top	3.349	3.509
4th	4.137	4.105
3rd	5.240	5.476
2nd	7.683	8.327
1st	13.475	14.4
Reverse	14.105	14.065

Suspension and steering
Rear suspension	Additional anti-roll bar
Wheels	Bolt on, cast alloy

Dimensions
Unladen weight   2,315lb/1050kg

MINI Cooper S
As for Mini One, except:

Engine
Compression ratio	8.3:1 (nominal)
Fuel supply	With mechanically-driven supercharger operating up to 0.8 Bar boost

Original:
Max. power	163bhp (DIN) @ 6,000rpm
Max. torque	155lb ft @ 4,000rpm

From Spring 2004:
Max. power	170bhp (DIN) at 6,000rpm
Max. torque	161lb ft @ 4,000rpm

Transmission (Manual)
Six-speed all-synchromesh gearbox by Getrag (Type 285)

Overall transmission ratios
Top	2.986
5th	3.656
4th	4.407
3rd	5.397
2nd	7.181
1st	11.425
Reverse	11.131

Transmission (Automatic)
From January 2005: Optional fixed-ratio six-speed automatic transmission, with Steptronic control available.

Suspension and steering
Rear	Additional anti-roll bar
Tyres	195/55-16 radial ply
Wheels	Bolt on, cast alloy
Rim width	5.0in on 16in wheels

Dimensions
Unladen weight   2,514lb/1140kg

MINI Cooper S 'Works'
As for MINI Cooper S, except:

Engine
Max. power	200bhp (DIN) @ 6,950rpm
Max. torque	177lb ft @ 4,000rpm

For 2005:
Max. power	210bhp (DIN) @ 6,950rpm
Max. torque	179lb ft @ 4,500rpm

Suspension and steering
Tyres	205/45-17 radial ply
Rim width	7.5in on 17in wheels

18in wheels also available

MINI ONE DIESEL

As for MINI One, except:

Engine

Type	BMW/Toyota
Block material	Cast aluminium
Bore and stroke	73 x 81.5mm
Capacity	1,364cc
Valves	4 per cylinder, operated by single overhead camshaft
Compression ratio	18.5:1
Fuel supply	Bosch common-rail fuel injection system and engine management system, with exhaust gas-driven turbocharger, and up to 0.5 Bar boost
Max. power	75bhp (DIN) @ 4,000rpm
Max. torque	132lb ft @ 2,000rpm

Transmission

Six-speed all-synchromesh manual gearbox by Getrag (Type 1285)

Overall transmission ratios

Top	2.41
5th	3.05
4th	3.55
3rd	4.51
2nd	6.99
1st	12.57
Reverse	11.13

Transmission (Automatic)

Not available on the diesel-engined MINI

Dimensions

Unladen weight	2,591lb/1175kg

Cabriolet

On announcement in 2004 the Cabriolet version, with convertible top, was available with the following mechanical packages:

One
Cooper
Cooper S

– but not available with the Diesel engine

All Cabriolets were 221lb/100kg heavier than their equivalent hatchback

114bhp from 1.6-litres – a bonnetful of power in the MINI Cooper.
(David Wigmore)

Index